MEXICAN
at home

Publications International, Ltd.

Pictured on the front cover: Fajita Pile-Ups *(page 62)*.
Pictured on the back cover *(clockwise from top left):* Pumpkin Flan *(page 168)*, Spicy Shrimp Sauté *(page 18)* and Beer and Chipotle Fish Tacos *(page 110)*.

ISBN-13: 978-1-60553-720-7
ISBN-10: 1-60553-720-9

Library of Congress Control Number: 2010924037

Manufactured in China.

8 7 6 5 4 3 2 1

Microwave Cooking: Microwave ovens vary in wattage. Use the cooking times as guidelines and check for doneness before adding more time.

Preparation/Cooking Times: Preparation times are based on the approximate amount of time required to assemble the recipe before cooking, baking, chilling or serving. These times include preparation steps such as measuring, chopping and mixing. The fact that some preparations and cooking can be done simultaneously is taken into account. Preparation of optional ingredients and serving suggestions is not included.

Publications International, Ltd.

Table of Contents

MENU

Ortega® Hot Poppers

Three Pepper Quesadillas

Classic Guacamole

Salsa Shrimp

Velveeta® Double-Decker Nachos

Chicken Empanaditas

Spicy Shrimp Sauté

Sopes

Cheesy Chorizo Wedges

Hearty Nachos

Cheesy Quesadillas

Zesty Appetizers

Ortega® Hot Poppers

1 can (3½ ounces) ORTEGA® Whole Jalapeños, drained
1 cup (4 ounces) shredded Cheddar cheese
1 package (3 ounces) cream cheese, softened
¼ cup chopped fresh cilantro
½ cup all-purpose flour
2 eggs, lightly beaten
2 cups cornflake cereal, crushed
   Vegetable oil
   ORTEGA® Salsa, any variety
   Sour cream

Cut jalapeños lengthwise into halves; remove seeds.

Blend Cheddar cheese, cream cheese and cilantro in small bowl. Place 1 to 1½ teaspoons cheese mixture into each jalapeño half; chill for 15 minutes or until cheese is firm.

Dip each jalapeño half in flour; shake off excess. Dip in eggs; coat with cornflake crumbs.

Add vegetable oil to 1-inch depth in medium skillet; heat over high heat for 1 minute. Fry jalapeños, turning frequently with tongs, until golden brown on all sides. Remove from skillet; drain on paper towels. Serve with salsa and sour cream. *Makes 8 servings*

Three Pepper Quesadillas

What You Need

- 1 cup *each* thin green, red and yellow bell pepper strips
- ½ cup thin onion slices
- ⅓ cup butter or margarine
- ½ teaspoon ground cumin
- 1 package (8 ounces) PHILADELPHIA® Cream Cheese, softened
- 1 package (8 ounces) KRAFT® Shredded Sharp Cheddar Cheese
- 10 TACO BELL® HOME ORIGINALS® Flour Tortillas
- 1 jar (16 ounces) TACO BELL® HOME ORIGINALS® Thick 'N Chunky Salsa

Make It

1. PREHEAT oven to 425°F. Cook and stir peppers and onion in butter in large skillet on medium-high heat until crisp-tender. Stir in cumin. Drain, reserving liquid.

2. BEAT cream cheese and Cheddar cheese with electric mixer on medium speed until well blended. Spoon 2 tablespoons cheese mixture onto each tortilla; top each evenly with pepper mixture. Fold tortillas in half; place on ungreased baking sheet. Brush with reserved liquid.

3. BAKE 10 minutes or until heated through. Cut each tortilla into thirds. Serve warm with salsa.   *Makes 30 servings, 1 piece each.*

Prep Time: 20 minutes
Bake Time: 10 minutes

Make Ahead: Prepare as directed except for baking; cover. Refrigerate. When ready to serve, bake, uncovered, at 425°F, 15 to 18 minutes or until thoroughly heated through.

Classic Guacamole

4 tablespoons finely chopped white onion, divided

1 to 2 serrano or jalapeño peppers, seeded and finely chopped

1 tablespoon plus 1½ teaspoons coarsely chopped fresh cilantro, divided

¼ teaspoon chopped garlic (optional)

2 large ripe avocados

1 medium tomato, peeled and chopped

1 to 2 teaspoons fresh lime juice

¼ teaspoon salt

Corn Tortilla Chips (recipe follows)

1. Combine 2 tablespoons onion, serranos, 1 tablespoon cilantro and garlic, if desired, in large mortar. Grind with pestle until almost smooth. (Mixture can be processed in food processor, if necessary, but it may become more watery than desired.)

2. Cut avocados lengthwise into halves; remove and discard pits. Scoop out avocado flesh; place in bowl. Add serrano mixture. Mash roughly, leaving avocado slightly chunky.

3. Add tomato, lime juice, salt and remaining 2 tablespoons onion and 1½ teaspoons cilantro to avocado mixture; mix well. Serve immediately or cover and refrigerate up to 4 hours. Serve with Corn Tortilla Chips.

Makes about 2 cups

Corn Tortilla Chips

12 (6-inch) corn tortillas, day-old*

Vegetable oil

½ to 1 teaspoon salt

*If tortillas are fresh, let stand, uncovered, in single layer on wire rack 1 to 2 hours to dry slightly.

continued on page 12

Classic Guacamole, continued

1. Stack 6 tortillas. Cutting through stack, cut into 6 equal wedges. Repeat with remaining tortillas.

2. Heat ½ inch oil in large heavy skillet over medium-high heat to 375°F; adjust heat to maintain temperature.

3. Fry tortilla wedges in single layer 1 minute or until crisp, turning occasionally. Remove and drain on paper towels. Sprinkle chips with salt. Repeat with remaining tortilla wedges.   *Makes 6 dozen*

Salsa Shrimp

- **1 cup chunky salsa**
- **1 can (4 ounces) diced mild green chiles**
- **2 teaspoons honey**
- **¼ teaspoon hot pepper sauce**
- **1 pound large cooked shrimp, peeled and deveined, with tails on**
  Chopped fresh cilantro, lemon wedges and sliced jalapeño pepper (optional)

1. Combine salsa, chiles, honey and hot pepper sauce in medium bowl; mix well. Add shrimp; toss to coat.

2. Cover; refrigerate 2 hours before serving. Garnish with cilantro, lemon and jalapeño.   *Makes about 6 servings*

Velveeta® Double-Decker Nachos

What You Need

- 6 ounces tortilla chips (about 7 cups)
- 1 can (15 ounces) chili with beans
- ½ pound (8 ounces) VELVEETA® Pasteurized Prepared Cheese Product, cut into ½-inch cubes
- 1 medium tomato, finely chopped
- ¼ cup sliced green onions
- ⅓ cup BREAKSTONE'S® or KNUDSEN® Sour Cream

Make It

1. ARRANGE half of the chips on large microwavable platter; top with layers of half each of the chili and VELVEETA®. Repeat layers.

2. MICROWAVE on HIGH 3 to 5 minutes or until VELVEETA® is melted.

3. TOP with remaining ingredients.   *Makes 6 servings*

Prep Time: 15 minutes
Total Time: 15 minutes

Variation: Prepare as directed, using VELVEETA® Mild Mexican Pasteurized Prepared Cheese Product with Jalapeño Peppers.

Chicken Empanaditas

Chicken Filling (recipe follows)
Pastry for double-crust 9-inch pie
1 egg yolk mixed with 1 teaspoon water

1. Preheat oven to 375°F. Prepare Chicken Filling.

2. Roll out pastry, one half at a time, on floured surface to ⅛-inch thickness; cut into 2½-inch circles. Place about 1 teaspoon Chicken Filling on each circle. Fold dough over to make half moons; seal edges with fork. Prick tops; brush with egg mixture.

3. Place on ungreased baking sheets. Bake 12 to 15 minutes or until golden brown. Serve warm. *Makes about 3 dozen*

Chicken Filling

1 tablespoon butter
1 cup finely chopped onion
2 cups finely chopped cooked chicken
¼ cup canned diced green chiles
1 tablespoon capers, drained and coarsely chopped
¼ teaspoon salt
1 cup (4 ounces) shredded Monterey Jack cheese

1. Melt butter in medium skillet over medium heat. Add onion; cook and stir until tender. Stir in chicken, chiles, capers and salt; cook 1 minute.

2. Remove from heat; stir in cheese. *Makes about 3 cups*

Spicy Shrimp Sauté

   2 tablespoons butter
   1 pound shrimp, peeled,* deveined
   ½ cup ORTEGA® Taco Sauce, any variety
   ½ cup ORTEGA® Salsa con Queso

*For easier handling and an attractive appearance, leave tails on.

Melt butter over medium heat in large skillet. Add shrimp; stir to coat with butter. Cook and stir 5 minutes or until shrimp turn pink.

Add taco sauce; stir to coat well. Cook 4 minutes or until sauce has thickened.

Microwave salsa on HIGH (100% power) for 30 seconds to warm. Serve with shrimp.   *Makes 4 servings*

Prep Time: 5 minutes
Start to Finish: 15 minutes

Variation: For an innovative appetizer, replace the shrimp with sea scallops; serve the scallops on toothpicks.

TIP

To devein shrimp, make a small cut along the back and lift out the dark vein with the tip of a knife. You may find this easier to do under cold running water.

Sopes

　4 cups masa harina flour

　½ cup vegetable shortening or lard

2½ cups warm water

　1 can (7 ounces) ORTEGA® Fire-Roasted Diced Green Chiles

　2 tablespoons vegetable oil, divided

Suggested Toppings

　　Warmed ORTEGA® Refried Beans, shredded mild Cheddar or
　　Monterey Jack cheese, ORTEGA® Salsa (any flavor), sour cream,
　　ORTEGA® Sliced Jalapeños

Place flour in large bowl; cut in vegetable shortening with pastry blender
or two knives until mixture resembles coarse crumbs. Gradually add water,
kneading until smooth. Add chiles; mix well. Form dough into 35 small
balls. Pat each ball into 3-inch patty; place on waxed paper.

Heat 1 teaspoon oil in large skillet over medium-high heat for 1 to
2 minutes. Cook patties for 3 minutes on each side or until golden brown,
adding additional oil as needed.

Top with beans, cheese, salsa, dollop of sour cream and jalapeños.

Makes about 35 servings

Cheesy Chorizo Wedges

Red & Green Salsa (recipe follows)
1 cup (4 ounces) shredded Monterey Jack cheese
1 cup (4 ounces) shredded mild Cheddar cheese
8 ounces chorizo
3 (10-inch) flour tortillas

1. Preheat oven to 450°F. Prepare Red & Green Salsa. Combine cheeses in small bowl.

2. Remove and discard casing from chorizo. Heat medium skillet over medium heat. Crumble chorizo into skillet. Brown 6 to 8 minutes, stirring to separate meat. Remove with slotted spoon; drain on paper towels.

3. Place tortillas on baking sheets. Divide chorizo evenly among tortillas, leaving ½ inch around edges uncovered. Sprinkle cheese mixture over top.

4. Bake 8 to 10 minutes or until edges are crisp and golden and cheese is bubbly and melted.

5. Cut each tortilla into 6 wedges. Serve with Red & Green Salsa.

Makes 6 to 8 servings

Red & Green Salsa

1 small red bell pepper, chopped
¼ cup coarsely chopped fresh cilantro
3 green onions, cut into thin slices
2 jalapeño peppers, seeded and minced
2 tablespoons fresh lime juice
1 clove garlic, minced
¼ teaspoon salt

1. Mix bell pepper, cilantro, green onions, jalapeños, lime juice, garlic and salt in small bowl. Let stand, covered, at room temperature 1 to 2 hours to blend flavors.

Makes 1 cup

Note: Jalapeño peppers can sting and irritate the skin, so wear rubber gloves when handling jalapeños and do not touch your eyes.

Hearty Nachos

1 pound ground beef
1 envelope LIPTON® RECIPE SECRETS® Onion Soup Mix
1 can (19 ounces) black beans, rinsed and drained
1 cup salsa
1 package (8½ ounces) plain tortilla chips
1 cup shredded Cheddar cheese (about 4 ounces)

1. In 12-inch nonstick skillet, brown ground beef over medium-high heat; drain.

2. Stir in soup mix, black beans and salsa. Bring to a boil over high heat. Reduce heat to low and simmer 5 minutes or until heated through.

3. Arrange tortilla chips on serving platter. Spread beef mixture over chips; sprinkle with Cheddar cheese. Top, if desired, with sliced green onions, sliced pitted ripe olives, chopped tomato and chopped cilantro.

Makes 8 servings

Prep Time: 10 minutes
Cook Time: 12 minutes

Cheesy Quesadillas

½ **pound ground beef**
1 **medium onion, chopped**
¼ **teaspoon salt**
1 **can (4½ ounces) chopped green chilies, drained**
1 **jar (1 pound 10 ounces) RAGÚ® Chunky Pasta Sauce, divided**
8 **(6½-inch) flour tortillas**
1 **tablespoon olive oil**
2 **cups shredded Cheddar and/or mozzarella cheese (about 8 ounces)**

1. Preheat oven to 400°F. In 12-inch skillet, brown ground beef with onion and salt over medium-high heat; drain. Stir in chilies and ½ cup Pasta Sauce; set aside.

2. Meanwhile, evenly brush one side of 4 tortillas with half of the olive oil. On cookie sheets, arrange tortillas, oil-side down. Evenly top with ½ of the cheese, beef filling, then remaining cheese. Top with remaining 4 tortillas, then brush tops with remaining oil.

3. Bake 10 minutes or until cheese is melted. To serve, cut each quesadilla into 4 wedges. Serve with remaining sauce, heated.   *Makes 4 servings*

Prep Time: 10 minutes
Cook Time: 15 minutes

Menu

Spinach Salad with Orange-Chili Glazed Shrimp

Chicken Tortilla and Rice Soup

Fajita Salad

Chipotle Black Bean Soup with Avocado Cream

Black Bean Mexicali Salad

Tortilla Soup

Layered Mexican Salad

New Mexican Pork Pozole

Taco Salad Supreme

Soups & Salads

Spinach Salad with Orange-Chili Glazed Shrimp

Orange-Chili Glazed Shrimp (recipe follows)

Dressing

- ¼ **cup orange juice**
- 1 **tablespoon cider vinegar**
- 2 **teaspoons toasted sesame seeds***
- 1 **clove garlic, minced**
- 1 **teaspoon** *each* **grated orange peel and olive oil**
- ½ **teaspoon honey**
- ⅛ **teaspoon red pepper flakes**

Salad

- 12 **cups packed torn stemmed spinach**
- 1 **large ripe mango, peeled and cubed**
- ½ **cup (2 ounces) crumbled feta cheese**

*To toast sesame seeds, spread in small skillet. Shake skillet over medium-low heat about 2 minutes or until seeds begin to pop and turn golden brown.

1. Prepare Orange-Chili Glazed Shrimp. Set aside.

2. For dressing, combine orange juice, vinegar, sesame seeds, garlic, orange peel, oil, honey and red pepper flakes in small bowl; mix well.

3. For salad, place spinach in large bowl; toss with dressing. Top with mango, cheese and shrimp.   *Makes 4 servings*

Orange-Chili Glazed Shrimp: Combine ½ cup orange juice, 2 teaspoons minced garlic and 1 teaspoon chili powder in large nonstick skillet. Bring to a boil over high heat. Boil 3 minutes or just until mixture coats bottom of skillet. Reduce heat to medium. Add 8 ounces large raw shrimp, peeled and deveined; cook and stir 2 minutes or until shrimp are pink and opaque. Makes 4 servings.

Chicken Tortilla and Rice Soup

2 cups MINUTE® White Rice, uncooked

5 cups low-sodium chicken broth

1 cup carrots, peeled and sliced thin

1 can (10 ounces) diced tomatoes with green chiles

1 cup (6 ounces) cooked chicken breast, cubed

1 tablespoon lime juice (optional)

20 baked tortilla chips (about 1 cup), slightly crushed

½ cup low-fat Mexican cheese blend, shredded

¼ cup fresh cilantro, chopped

1 avocado, diced (optional)

Prepare rice according to package directions.

Bring broth to a boil in medium pot. Reduce heat and add carrots, tomatoes with chiles and chicken; simmer 10 minutes.

Stir in rice; add lime juice, if desired. Divide equally into 6 serving bowls and top with tortilla chips, cheese, cilantro and avocado, if desired.

Makes 6 servings

TIP

To dice an avocado, insert a knife into the stem end. Slice in half lengthwise to the pit, turning while slicing. Twist the halves in opposite directions to pull apart. Press the knife into the pit, twisting gently to pull the pit from the avocado; discard. Cut the flesh in a crisscross fashion and run a spoon underneath the pieces.

Fajita Salad

¼ cup fresh lime juice

2 tablespoons chopped fresh cilantro

1 clove garlic, minced

1 teaspoon chili powder

½ boneless beef top sirloin steak (6 ounces), cut into strips

1 teaspoon olive oil

2 medium red bell peppers, cut into strips

1 medium onion, sliced

1 cup canned chickpeas, rinsed and drained

4 cups mixed salad greens

1 medium tomato, cut into wedges

1 cup salsa

1. Combine lime juice, cilantro, garlic and chili powder in large resealable food storage bag. Add beef; seal bag. Let stand 10 minutes, turning once.

2. Heat oil in large nonstick skillet over medium-high heat. Add bell peppers and onion; cook and stir 6 minutes or until vegetables are crisp-tender. Remove from skillet.

3. Add beef and marinade to skillet; cook and stir 3 minutes or until beef is cooked through. Remove from heat. Add bell pepper mixture and chickpeas to skillet; toss to coat with pan juices. Cool slightly.

4. Divide salad greens evenly among serving plates. Top with beef mixture and tomato wedges. Serve with salsa.

Makes 4 servings

Chipotle Black Bean Soup with Avocado Cream

2 tablespoons olive oil

4 large carrots, diced (about 2 cups)

1 large sweet onion, diced (about 2 cups)

2 cloves garlic, minced

1 canned chipotle chili pepper in adobo sauce, minced*

4 cups SWANSON® Chicken Broth (Regular, Natural Goodness® or Certified Organic)

3 cans (about 15 ounces each) black beans, rinsed and drained

1 small ripe avocado, pitted, peeled and cut into cubes (about ½ cup)

¼ cup sour cream

2 tablespoons chopped fresh cilantro leaves

1 tablespoon lemon juice

*For a less spicy soup, use **half** of a chipotle chili pepper.

1. Heat the oil in a 4-quart saucepan. Add the carrots and onion and cook until tender-crisp. Add the garlic and pepper and cook for 1 minute. Add the broth and beans and heat to a boil. Reduce the heat to low. Cook for 25 minutes.

2. Mash the avocado with a fork in a small bowl until smooth. Stir in the sour cream, cilantro and lemon juice and set it aside.

3. Spoon ⅓ of the soup mixture into an electric blender or food processor container. Cover and blend until smooth. Pour the mixture into a large bowl. Repeat the blending process twice more with the remaining broth

continued on page 36

Chipotle Black Bean Soup with Avocado Cream, continued

mixture. Return all the puréed mixture to the saucepan. Cook over medium heat until the mixture is hot. Season to taste. Divide the soup among 8 serving bowls. Top each serving of soup with the avocado cream.

Makes 8 servings

Prep Time: 10 minutes
Cook Time: 40 minutes

Note: Chipotle chili peppers in adobo sauce are sold in cans and may be found in the Mexican or ethnic food section of grocery stores.

Black Bean Mexicali Salad

1 can (about 15 ounces) black beans, rinsed and drained
1 cup fresh or thawed frozen corn
6 ounces roasted red bell peppers, cut into thin strips
½ cup chopped red or yellow onion
⅓ cup mild chipotle or regular salsa
2 tablespoons cider vinegar
2 ounces mozzarella cheese, cut into ¼-inch cubes
Chopped fresh cilantro (optional)

1. Place beans, corn, bell peppers, onion, salsa and vinegar in medium bowl; toss gently. Let stand 15 minutes to blend flavors.

2. Just before serving, gently fold in cheese. Garnish with cilantro.

Makes 6 servings

Tortilla Soup

Vegetable oil
3 (6- or 7-inch) corn tortillas, halved and cut into strips
½ cup chopped onion
1 clove garlic, minced
2 cans (about 14 ounces each) chicken broth
1 can (about 14 ounces) diced tomatoes
1 cup shredded cooked chicken
2 teaspoons fresh lime juice
1 small avocado, diced
2 tablespoons chopped fresh cilantro

1. Pour oil to depth of ½ inch in small skillet. Heat over medium-high heat until oil reaches 360°F on deep-fry thermometer. Add tortilla strips, a few at a time; fry 1 minute or until crisp and lightly browned. Remove with slotted spoon; drain on paper towels.

2. Heat 2 teaspoons oil in large saucepan over medium heat. Add onion and garlic; cook and stir until onion is soft. Add broth and tomatoes; bring to a boil. Cover; reduce heat and simmer 15 minutes.

3. Add chicken and lime juice; simmer 5 minutes. Top soup with tortilla strips, avocado and cilantro.   *Makes 4 servings*

Layered Mexican Salad

⅔ cup dried black beans *or* 1 can (about 15 ounces) black beans, rinsed and drained

1 small head romaine lettuce, cut into strips

1½ cups salsa

1 cup frozen corn, thawed and drained

1 large cucumber, peeled and sliced

1 can (2¼ ounces) sliced black olives, drained

¾ cup mayonnaise

Grated peel and juice of 1 large lemon

3 tablespoons plain yogurt

2 to 3 cloves garlic, minced

½ cup (2 ounces) shredded Cheddar cheese

1 green onion, thinly sliced

1. Rinse and sort dried beans. Place in medium saucepan with 4 cups water. Bring to a boil over high heat. Reduce heat to medium-low; simmer 5 minutes. Remove from heat; cover and let stand 1 to 2 hours.

2. Drain beans. Return to saucepan with 4 cups fresh water. Bring to a boil over high heat. Reduce heat to medium-low; cover and simmer 1½ to 2 hours or until tender. Drain; rinse and drain again.

3. Place half of lettuce in large serving bowl. Layer salsa, beans and corn over lettuce. Place cucumber on top of corn; sprinkle with olives. Top with remaining lettuce.

4. Blend mayonnaise, lemon peel, lemon juice, yogurt and garlic in small bowl. Spread dressing evenly on top of salad. Sprinkle with cheese and green onion. Cover salad and refrigerate 2 hours or up to 1 day.

Makes 12 servings

New Mexican Pork Pozole

1 cup dried lima beans, rinsed and sorted

2 tablespoons vegetable oil

1 pound pork tenderloin, cut into 1-inch cubes

1½ cups chopped onions

3 cloves garlic, minced

2 cups chicken broth

1 can (about 14 ounces) diced tomatoes

2 bay leaves

1 teaspoon ground cumin

1 teaspoon ground coriander

½ teaspoon red pepper flakes

1 can (16 ounces) yellow hominy, drained

3 medium zucchini, diced

Hot cooked brown rice

1. Place beans in medium saucepan and cover with 4 inches of water. Bring to a boil over high heat; boil 2 minutes. Remove from heat; cover and let stand 1 hour.

2. Heat oil in Dutch oven over medium-high heat. Add pork; cook until browned, stirring frequently. Remove pork with slotted spoon; set aside.

3. Add onions and garlic to Dutch oven; cook and stir 3 minutes or until onions are tender.

4. Drain beans; add to onion mixture. Add pork, broth, tomatoes, bay leaves, cumin, coriander and red pepper flakes. Bring to a boil over high heat. Reduce heat to low; simmer, partially covered, 1½ hours.

5. Add hominy and zucchini to bean mixture; simmer, covered, 25 to 30 minutes or until beans are tender. Remove bay leaves; discard. Spoon hot rice into serving bowls. Top with pozole.   *Makes 6 to 8 servings*

Taco Salad Supreme

1 pound ground beef
½ cup chopped onion
2 cloves garlic, minced
1 teaspoon ground cumin
1 teaspoon chili powder
½ teaspoon salt
½ cup salsa, divided
6 cups packed torn or sliced romaine lettuce
1 large tomato, chopped
1 cup (4 ounces) shredded Mexican cheese blend
   or taco cheese blend, divided
1 ripe avocado, diced
¼ cup sour cream

1. Brown beef with onion 6 to 8 minutes in large skillet over medium-high heat, stirring to break up meat. Drain fat. Add garlic, cumin, chili powder and salt; cook 1 minute, stirring frequently. Stir in ¼ cup salsa; cook and stir 1 minute. Remove from heat.

2. Combine lettuce, tomato, ½ cup cheese and remaining ¼ cup salsa in large bowl; toss well. Divide salad among serving plates. Spoon meat mixture evenly over salads; top with remaining ½ cup cheese, avocado and sour cream.

Makes 4 servings

MENU

- Gridiron Cheddar & Garlic Steak Fajitas
- Margarita Pork Kabobs
- Grilled Strip Steaks with Fresh Chimichurri
- Beef Enchiladas
- Roasted Pork in Pineapple-Chile Adobo
- Carne Asada
- Pork Tacos with Roasted Green Onions
- Cheesy Chimichangas
- Fajita Pile-Ups
- Enchilada Slow-Roasted Baby Back Ribs
- Overstuffed Mexican-Style Peppers
- Zesty Steak Fajitas
- Spicy Meat Tostadas
- Mexicali Burgers
- Soft Tacos
- Mexican-Style Steak and Peppers

Beef & Pork

Gridiron Cheddar & Garlic Steak Fajitas

- 1 tablespoon olive oil
- 2 large red, orange or yellow peppers, cut into 2-inch-long strips (about 4 cups)
- 1 large sweet onion, thinly sliced (about 1 cup)
- 2 cloves garlic, minced
- 1½ pounds skirt or boneless beef sirloin steak, ½ to ¾ inch thick, cut into very thin strips
- 1 can (10¾ ounces) CAMPBELL'S® Condensed Cheddar Cheese Soup
- 1 tablespoon lime juice
- 6 flour tortillas (8-inch), warmed
- 1 jar (15 ounces) PACE® Chunky Salsa

  Optional Toppings: Shredded Cheddar cheese, chopped avocado, hot pepper sauce, sour cream and shredded lettuce

  Lime wedges (optional)

1. Heat the oil in a deep 12-inch skillet over medium-high heat. Add the peppers and onion and cook until the vegetables are tender. Add the garlic and cook for 30 seconds. Remove the vegetable mixture from the skillet with a slotted spoon and set it aside.

2. Add the steak in 2 batches and cook and stir until it's well browned. Remove the steak with a slotted spoon and set it aside.

3. Add the soup and lime juice. Heat to a boil. Return the vegetables and beef to the skillet and cook until the mixture is hot and bubbling.

4. Spoon about ¼ cup steak mixture down the center of each tortilla. Top with salsa and toppings, if desired. Serve with lime wedges, if desired.

Makes 6 servings

Prep Time: 15 minutes
Cook Time: 15 minutes

Margarita Pork Kabobs

1 cup margarita drink mix or 1 cup lime juice, 4 teaspoons sugar and
     ½ teaspoon salt
1 teaspoon ground coriander
1 clove garlic, minced
1 pound pork tenderloin, cut into 1-inch cubes
2 tablespoons margarine, melted
1 tablespoon minced fresh parsley
2 teaspoons lime juice
⅛ teaspoon sugar
1 large green or red bell pepper, cut into 1-inch cubes
2 ears corn, cut into 8 pieces

For marinade, combine margarita mix, coriander and garlic in small
bowl. Place pork cubes in large resealable plastic food storage bag; pour
marinade over pork. Close bag securely; turn to coat. Marinate for at least
30 minutes. Combine margarine, parsley, lime juice and sugar in small
bowl; set aside. Thread pork cubes onto four skewers, alternating with
pieces of bell pepper and corn. (If using bamboo skewers, soak in water
20 to 30 minutes before using to prevent them from burning.) Grill over
hot coals for 15 to 20 minutes or until barely pink in center, basting with
margarine mixture and turning frequently.   *Makes 4 servings*

Favorite recipe from **National Pork Board**

Grilled Strip Steaks with Fresh Chimichurri

4 (8-ounce) bone-in strip steaks, about 1 inch thick
¾ teaspoon salt
¾ teaspoon ground cumin
¼ teaspoon black pepper
Chimichurri (recipe follows)

1. Spray grid with nonstick cooking spray. Prepare grill for direct cooking. Sprinkle both sides of each steak with salt, cumin and pepper.

2. Grill steaks over medium-high heat, covered, 8 to 10 minutes for medium rare or until desired doneness, turning once. Serve with Chimichurri.

Makes 4 servings

Chimichurri

½ cup packed fresh basil
⅓ cup extra virgin olive oil
¼ cup packed fresh parsley
2 tablespoons packed fresh cilantro
2 tablespoons fresh lemon juice
1 clove garlic
½ teaspoon salt
½ teaspoon grated orange peel
¼ teaspoon ground coriander
⅛ teaspoon black pepper

1. Place all ingredients in food processor or blender; purée.

Makes about 1 cup

Beef Enchiladas

Red Chile Sauce (page 53)
2 tablespoons vegetable oil
1½ pounds boneless beef chuck shoulder, cut into 1-inch cubes
½ teaspoon salt
½ cup finely chopped white onion
¾ cup beef broth
¼ cup raisins
1 clove garlic, minced
½ teaspoon ground cloves
¼ teaspoon anise seeds, crushed
12 (6-inch) corn tortillas
1 cup (4 ounces) shredded mild Cheddar cheese
¾ cup sour cream
⅓ cup sliced pitted black olives

1. Prepare Red Chile Sauce. Heat oil in large skillet over medium heat. Sprinkle beef with salt. Brown beef in batches 10 to 12 minutes; remove to plate.

2. Add onion to skillet; cook and stir 4 minutes or until onion is tender. Return beef to skillet. Stir in broth, raisins, ¼ cup Red Chile Sauce, garlic, cloves and anise seeds. Bring to a boil over medium-high heat. Reduce heat to low. Cover and simmer 1½ to 2 hours or until beef is very tender. Remove from heat. Using 2 forks, pull beef into coarse shreds in skillet.*

3. Preheat oven to 375°F. Heat remaining Red Chile Sauce in medium skillet over medium heat; remove from heat.

4. Dip 1 tortilla in sauce with tongs a few seconds or until limp. Drain off excess sauce. Spread about 3 tablespoons meat filling down center of tortilla. Roll up; place in 13×9-inch baking dish. Repeat with remaining tortillas, sauce and meat filling. Pour remaining sauce over enchiladas; sprinkle with cheese.

5. Bake 25 minutes or until bubbly and cheese is melted. To serve, spoon sour cream down center of enchiladas. Sprinkle with olives.

Makes 4 to 6 servings

*Beef mixture can be frozen at this point. Store in large resealable freezer bags. Thaw in refrigerator before proceeding as directed.

Red Chile Sauce

  3 ounces dried ancho chiles (about 5), seeded, deveined and rinsed
2½ cups boiling water
  2 tablespoons tomato paste
  2 tablespoons vegetable oil
  1 clove garlic, minced
  ½ teaspoon salt
  ½ teaspoon dried oregano
  ¼ teaspoon ground cumin
  ¼ teaspoon ground coriander

1. Place chiles in medium bowl; cover with boiling water. Let stand 1 hour.

2. Place chiles along with soaking water in blender; blend until smooth.

3. Whisk chile mixture, tomato paste, oil, garlic, salt, oregano, cumin and coriander in medium saucepan. Bring to a boil. Reduce heat. Cover and simmer 10 minutes, stirring occasionally.

Makes about 2½ cups

Note: Sauce can be covered and refrigerated up to 3 days or frozen up to 1 month.

Roasted Pork in Pineapple-Chile Adobo

1 fresh DOLE® Tropical Gold® Pineapple
3 tablespoons packed brown sugar, divided
1 to 2 tablespoons chopped canned chipotle peppers
2 tablespoons lime juice
1 tablespoon yellow mustard
2 teaspoons dried oregano leaves, crushed
¼ teaspoon ground black pepper
1½ pounds pork tenderloin
    Lime wedges

• Twist off crown from pineapple. Cut fresh pineapple in half lengthwise. Cut one pineapple half crosswise into 1-inch thick slices. Cut remaining portion in half. Refrigerate one quarter for another use. Core, skin and finely chop remaining quarter. Set aside.

• Arrange fresh pineapple slices in single layer on large baking sheet. Sprinkle with half of sugar. Set aside.

• Combine chopped fresh pineapple, peppers, lime juice, mustard, oregano and black pepper in shallow roasting pan. Add pork; spoon mixture over pork to cover all sides.

• Bake pork and pineapple at 400°F, 40 to 50 minutes until pork is no longer pink in center and fresh pineapple is golden, turning pineapple halfway through cooking and sprinkling with remaining sugar. Let pork stand 5 minutes. Slice pork into ½-inch-thick slices. Serve with fresh pineapple and lime wedges.   *Makes 6 servings*

Prep Time: 15 minutes
Bake Time: 50 minutes

Carne Asada

rt steaks

cheese

ne juice and garlic in
g, turning to coat.

arinade. Place
tes. Grill steaks
f marinade.
nedium rare

ill

Cheesy Chimichangas

1½ **pounds lean ground beef**

2 **large onions, chopped**

2 **teaspoons garlic salt**

½ **teaspoon black pepper**

8 **(8-inch) ORTEGA® Soft Flour Tortillas**

2 **tablespoons vegetable oil, divided**

1 **jar (16 ounces) ORTEGA® Salsa, any variety, divided**

2 **cups (8 ounces) shredded Cheddar cheese, divided**

2 **cups (8 ounces) shredded Monterey Jack cheese, divided**

Shredded lettuce and chopped tomatoes

1 **jar (11.5 ounces) ORTEGA® Guacamole Style Dip**

Preheat oven to 450°F. Grease or lightly coat 13×9-inch baking dish with nonstick cooking spray; set aside.

Cook and stir beef and onions in large skillet over medium-high heat until no longer pink. Drain and discard fat. Stir in garlic salt and pepper.

Brush one side of each tortilla with oil. Spoon ¼ cup beef mixture off-center on oiled side of each tortilla. Top each with 1 tablespoon salsa, 1 tablespoon Cheddar cheese and 1 tablespoon Monterey Jack cheese. Fold ends of tortilla to middle, then roll tightly around mixture. Place in prepared baking dish. Repeat with remaining tortillas. Brush tops with remaining oil.

Bake, uncovered, 10 to 15 minutes or until lightly browned. Sprinkle with remaining cheeses. Bake 2 to 3 minutes longer or until cheese is melted.

Serve warm on bed of lettuce and tomatoes. Spoon remaining salsa over chimichangas. Serve with guacamole. *Makes 8 servings*

Prep Time: 25 minutes
Start to Finish: 40 minutes

Fajita Pile-Ups

2 teaspoons vegetable oil, divided

12 ounces sirloin steak, trimmed of fat, cut into thin strips

2 teaspoons steak seasoning

½ medium lime

1 medium green bell pepper, cut into ½-inch strips

1 medium red or yellow bell pepper, cut into ½-inch strips

1 large onion, cut into ½-inch wedges, layers separated

1 cup cherry tomatoes, halved

½ teaspoon ground cumin

4 (6-inch) corn tortillas

Sour cream and chopped fresh cilantro (optional)

Lime wedges (optional)

1. Heat 1 teaspoon oil in large nonstick skillet over medium-high heat. Add steak; sprinkle with seasoning. Cook and stir 3 minutes or just until slightly pink in center. *Do not overcook.* Transfer to plate. Squeeze ½ lime over steak. Cover to keep warm.

2. Add remaining 1 teaspoon oil to skillet. Add bell peppers and onion; cook and stir 8 minutes or just until tender. Add tomatoes; cook and stir 1 minute. Return steak with any accumulated juices and cumin to skillet; cook and stir 1 minute.

3. Warm tortillas according to package directions. Top each tortilla evenly with steak mixture. Garnish with sour cream and cilantro. Serve open-faced with lime wedges, if desired.

Makes 4 servings

Enchilada Slow-Roasted Baby Back Ribs

1 packet (1.25 ounces) ORTEGA® Fajita Seasoning Mix
¼ cup packed brown sugar
4 slabs baby back ribs (about 10 pounds)
½ cup Dijon mustard
2 jars (8 ounces each) ORTEGA® Enchilada Sauce

Preheat oven to 250°F. Combine seasoning mix and brown sugar in small bowl. Place large piece of aluminum foil on counter. On foil, brush both sides of ribs with mustard; sprinkle both sides with seasoning mixture.

Adjust one oven rack to low position. Remove remaining oven rack; arrange ribs on rack. Slide rack with ribs into upper-middle position in oven. Place foil-lined baking sheet on lower rack to collect drippings from ribs.

Roast ribs 1½ to 2 hours or until tender. Remove ribs from oven. Turn on broiler.

Brush enchilada sauce onto both sides of ribs. Transfer ribs to foil-lined baking sheet, meat side down. Broil 5 to 6 minutes or until sauce begins to bubble. Let stand 5 minutes before slicing into individual servings.

Makes 6 to 8 servings

Prep Time: 15 minutes
Start to Finish: 2 hours

Tip: You can also grill the ribs. Follow the same procedures, keeping the grill temperature at about 250°F and grill with the cover on.

Overstuffed Mexican-Style Peppers

10 ounces ground beef

½ cup finely chopped onion

1 can (4 ounces) chopped mild green chiles

½ cup corn

½ cup tomato sauce, divided

¼ cup cornmeal

½ teaspoon salt

½ teaspoon ground cumin

2 large green bell peppers, cut in half lengthwise, seeded and stemmed

⅔ cup (about 2½ ounces) shredded Cheddar cheese

1. Preheat oven to 375°F.

2. Brown beef 6 to 8 minutes in medium nonstick skillet over medium-high heat, stirring to break up meat. Drain fat. Add onion, chiles, corn, ¼ cup tomato sauce, cornmeal, salt and cumin; mix well.

3. Arrange pepper halves, cut side up, in 12×8-inch baking pan. Spoon beef mixture evenly into each pepper half. Spoon remaining ¼ cup tomato sauce over beef mixture.

4. Bake about 35 minutes or until peppers are tender. Sprinkle with cheese. Serve immediately.   *Makes 4 servings*

Zesty Steak Fajitas

¾ cup *French's*® Worcestershire Sauce, divided

1 pound boneless top round, sirloin or flank steak

3 tablespoons taco seasoning mix

2 red or green bell peppers, cut into quarters

1 to 2 large onions, cut into thick slices

¾ cup chili sauce

8 (8-inch) flour or corn tortillas, heated

Sour cream and shredded cheese (optional)

1. Pour *½ cup* Worcestershire over steak in deep dish. Cover and refrigerate 30 minutes or up to 3 hours. Drain meat and rub both sides with seasoning mix. Discard marinade.

2. Grill meat and vegetables over medium-hot coals 10 to 15 minutes until meat is medium-rare and vegetables are charred, but tender.

3. Thinly slice meat and vegetables. Place in large bowl. Add chili sauce and remaining *¼ cup* Worcestershire. Toss to coat. Serve in tortillas and garnish with sour cream and cheese.

Makes 4 servings

Prep Time: 5 minutes
Cook Time: 15 minutes
Marinate Time: 30 minutes

Spicy Meat Tostadas

8 ounces ground beef

4 ounces ground pork

½ cup chopped onion

1 jalapeño pepper, seeded and minced

1 clove garlic, minced

½ cup canned diced tomatoes, drained

1 tablespoon cider vinegar

1 teaspoon *each* brown sugar and chili powder

¼ teaspoon *each* salt, ground cumin and dried oregano

⅛ teaspoon ground cinnamon

8 (6- or 7-inch) corn tortillas

1 can (about 15 ounces) refried beans, warmed

2 cups shredded lettuce

1 cup (4 ounces) shredded Cheddar or Monterey Jack cheese

1 large avocado, sliced

2 tomatoes, coarsely chopped

1 small onion, thinly sliced crosswise and separated into rings

1 cup salsa or picante sauce

1. Brown beef and pork in large skillet over medium-high heat. Add chopped onion, jalapeño and garlic. Reduce heat to medium; cook and stir until onion is tender. Spoon off and discard pan drippings. Add diced tomatoes, vinegar, sugar, chili powder, salt, cumin, oregano and cinnamon. Simmer, stirring occasionally, 15 minutes or until most liquid has evaporated.

2. Meanwhile, preheat oven to 400°F. Place tortillas in single layer directly on oven rack. Bake 10 to 12 minutes or until crisp.

3. Spread tortillas evenly with refried beans, meat mixture, lettuce, cheese, avocado, chopped tomatoes and sliced onion. Drizzle with salsa.

Makes 8 tostadas

Mexicali Burgers

Guacamole (recipe follows)
1 pound ground beef
⅓ cup crushed tortilla chips
⅓ cup salsa or picante sauce
3 tablespoons finely chopped fresh cilantro
2 tablespoons finely chopped onion
1 teaspoon ground cumin
4 slices Monterey Jack or Cheddar cheese
4 kaiser rolls or hamburger buns, split
Lettuce leaves and sliced tomatoes

1. Spray grid with nonstick cooking spray. Prepare grill for direct cooking. Prepare Guacamole.

2. Combine beef, tortilla chips, salsa, cilantro, onion and cumin in medium bowl until well blended. Shape mixture into 4 burgers. Grill over medium heat, covered, 8 to 10 minutes (or, uncovered, 13 to 15 minutes) to medium (160°F), turning once. Place 1 slice cheese on each burger during last 1 to 2 minutes of grilling. If desired, place rolls, cut side down, on grill to toast lightly during last 1 to 2 minutes of grilling.

3. Place burgers between rolls; top with Guacamole. Serve with lettuce and tomatoes. *Makes 4 servings*

Guacamole: Place 1 ripe avocado in medium bowl; mash with fork until slightly chunky. Add 1 tablespoon salsa, 1 teaspoon lime juice and ¼ teaspoon garlic salt; blend well. Makes about ½ cup.

Soft Tacos

1 pound ground beef
1 package (1.25 ounces) taco seasoning mix
¾ cup water
8 flour tortillas (8-inch), warmed
1 cup PACE® Picante Sauce
1 cup shredded iceberg lettuce
1 cup shredded Cheddar cheese (4 ounces)

1. Cook the beef in a 10-inch skillet over medium-high heat until the beef is well browned, stirring frequently to separate meat. Pour off any fat.

2. Stir the taco seasoning mix and water into the skillet. Heat to a boil. Reduce the heat to low. Cook for 5 minutes.

3. Spoon about ¼ cup beef mixture down center of each tortilla. Divide the picante sauce, lettuce and cheese among the tortillas. Fold the tortilla around the filling. Serve with additional picante sauce.   *Makes 8 tacos*

Prep/Cook Time: 15 minutes

Mexican-Style Steak and Peppers

1 jar (16 ounces) salsa
½ cup vegetable oil
   Juice of 2 limes
1 teaspoon chili powder
¼ teaspoon onion powder
1½ pounds boneless beef top sirloin steak
3 red, green and/or yellow bell peppers, quartered
1 red onion, cut into thick rings

1. Combine salsa, oil, lime juice, chili powder and onion powder in medium bowl; mix well.

2. Place steak, bell peppers and onion in large resealable food storage bag. Add 1 cup salsa mixture; turn to coat. Marinate in refrigerator 1 to 8 hours, turning occasionally. Refrigerate remaining salsa mixture.

3. Prepare grill for direct cooking. Remove steak and vegetables from marinade; discard marinade. Grill steak and vegetables over medium-high heat, covered, 8 to 10 minutes or until steak reaches desired doneness and vegetables are tender, turning once.

4. Meanwhile, heat remaining salsa mixture in small saucepan over low heat, stirring occasionally. Cut steak into ¼-inch-thick slices. Top steak and vegetables with salsa mixture. *Makes 4 to 6 servings*

Variation: You may substitute 1 beef flank steak or 4 top loin steaks.

Menu

Chicken Burritos

Easy Chicken and Rice Tacos

Chicken Flautas with Tomatillo Salsa

Black Bean Garnachas

Tropical Chipotle Chicken Skewers

Tacos Dorados

Mole Chicken

Chicken Fajitas

Chicken and Bean Tostadas

Chipotle Chicken Taquitos

Chicken & Spinach Quesadillas
with Pico de Gallo

Grilled Chicken with Corn
and Black Bean Salsa

Creamy Enchiladas Verde

Chicken Fiesta

Chicken Fiesta

Chicken Burritos

2 cups chicken broth

1 cup uncooked white rice

1 can (about 15 ounces) black beans, rinsed and drained

1 can (about 14 ounces) diced tomatoes

1 cup shredded cooked chicken

10 (6-inch) flour tortillas, warmed

   Taco or enchilada sauce, sour cream, shredded lettuce
     and red chile slices

   Guacamole and salsa (optional)

1. Combine broth and rice in medium saucepan; bring to a boil over high heat. Reduce heat to a simmer; simmer 10 minutes or until rice is tender.

2. Add beans, tomatoes and chicken; cook 10 minutes or until mixture is heated through.

3. Divide mixture evenly among tortillas. Top with taco sauce, sour cream, lettuce and chiles. Serve with guacamole and salsa, if desired.

Makes 10 servings

TIP

To warm tortillas, stack 8 to 10 and wrap them in plastic wrap. Microwave on HIGH 40 to 50 seconds, turning over and rotating ¼ turn once during heating. For only 1 or 2 tortillas, wrap and heat on HIGH about 20 seconds.

Chicken Fiesta

Easy Chicken and Rice Tacos

 1 tablespoon butter or margarine
 1 pound ground chicken
 1 small onion, chopped
 1 packet (1¼ ounces) taco seasoning mix
1¼ cups water
 1 can (8 ounces) tomato sauce
1½ cups MINUTE® White Rice, uncooked
 1 can (15 ounces) kidney beans, drained and rinsed
16 taco shells, heated
 1 package (8 ounces) Cheddar cheese, shredded
 1 cup lettuce, shredded
 2 medium tomatoes, chopped

Melt butter in large skillet over medium-high heat. Add chicken and onion; cook and stir until chicken is cooked through.

Stir in seasoning mix, water and tomato sauce. Bring to a boil. Reduce heat to low; cover. Simmer 5 minutes.

Add rice and beans; mix well. Cover; remove from heat. Let stand 5 minutes.

Fill taco shells evenly with chicken mixture; top with cheese, lettuce and tomatoes.

Makes 8 servings

Chicken Fiesta

Chicken Flautas with Tomatillo Salsa

1½ pounds tomatillos, husks removed, rinsed and patted dry
1 jalapeño pepper, stemmed
½ medium red onion, cut into ½-inch wedges
2 cloves garlic
¾ cup chopped fresh cilantro, divided
1½ teaspoons salt, divided
    Lime juice to taste
3 cups water
1 pound boneless skinless chicken breast
2 bay leaves
½ cup picante sauce
½ teaspoon ground cumin
1 cup vegetable oil
16 (6-inch) corn tortillas

1. Preheat broiler. Broil tomatillos, jalapeño, onion and garlic 10 minutes or until tomatillos are softened and lightly charred, turning twice. Place tomatillo mixture, ½ cup cilantro and 1 teaspoon salt in food processor or blender; purée. Cool. Stir in lime juice and remaining ¼ cup cilantro.

2. Bring water to a boil in large saucepan over high heat. Add chicken, bay leaves and remaining ½ teaspoon salt; bring to a boil. Reduce heat; cover and simmer 15 minutes or until chicken is no longer pink in center. Remove from saucepan, reserving ¼ cup water in saucepan; discard bay leaves. Shred chicken; return to saucepan. Add picante sauce and cumin; stir.

3. Preheat oven to 425°F. Heat oil in large skillet over medium heat. Cook tortillas, one at a time, 5 seconds on each side; drain. Spoon chicken evenly on one end of each tortilla; roll tightly. Place, seam side down, on baking sheet. Bake 15 minutes or until golden. Serve with salsa.

Makes 16 flautas

Black Bean Garnachas

1 can (14½ ounces) DEL MONTE® Diced Tomatoes with Garlic & Onion

1 can (15 ounces) black or pinto beans, drained

2 cloves garlic, minced

1 to 2 teaspoons minced jalapeño peppers (optional)

½ teaspoon ground cumin

1 cup cubed grilled chicken

4 flour tortillas

½ cup (2 ounces) shredded sharp Cheddar cheese

1. Combine undrained tomatoes, beans, garlic, jalapeño peppers and cumin in large skillet. Cook over medium-high heat 5 to 7 minutes or until thickened, stirring occasionally. Stir in chicken. Season with salt and pepper, if desired.

2. Arrange tortillas in single layer on grill over medium coals. Spread about ¾ cup chicken mixture over each tortilla. Top with cheese.

3. Cook about 3 minutes or until bottoms of tortillas are browned and cheese is melted. Top with shredded lettuce, diced avocado and sliced jalapeño peppers, if desired.

Makes 4 servings

Prep Time: 5 minutes
Cook Time: 10 minutes

Variation: Prepare chicken mixture as directed above. Place a tortilla in a dry skillet over medium heat. Spread with about ¾ cup chicken mixture; top with 2 tablespoons cheese. Cover and cook about 3 minutes or until bottom of tortilla is browned and cheese is melted. Repeat with remaining tortillas.

Tropical Chipotle Chicken Skewers

¾ cup low-sodium ketchup

½ cup pineapple juice

3 canned chipotle chilies in adobo sauce

2 teaspoons minced garlic

½ cup chopped fresh cilantro

1½ pounds boneless, skinless chicken breast, cut into 1½-inch cubes

32 (about 1 cup) California Ripe Olives, whole, pitted

1 cup cubed pineapple (1-inch)

8 (12-inch) wooden skewers, soaked in warm water

Process ketchup, pineapple juice, chilies and garlic in bowl of food processor. Stir in cilantro. Reserve 1 cup sauce for dipping. Pour remaining chipotle sauce into large bowl and combine with chicken. Cover; refrigerate to marinate for 15 to 30 minutes. Prepare skewers by threading each with a California Ripe Olive, pineapple chunk and a piece of marinated chicken. Repeat pattern 2 times, then finish each skewer with 1 more California Ripe Olive. Grill skewers over medium-high heat for 7 to 9 minutes, turning to cook evenly. Serve 2 skewers on each plate accompanied with ¼ cup of dipping sauce.   *Makes 4 servings*

Favorite recipe from *California Olive Industry*

Tacos Dorados

2 tablespoons vegetable oil

1¾ pounds boneless skinless chicken breasts, cut into 1-inch cubes

½ cup chopped onion

1 can (about 28 ounces) diced tomatoes

2 teaspoons chili powder

1 teaspoon ground cumin

½ teaspoon salt

½ teaspoon garlic powder

½ teaspoon dried oregano

¼ teaspoon ground coriander

10 (8-inch) flour tortillas

3½ cups (14 ounces) shredded queso blanco*

¼ cup chopped fresh cilantro

Salsa and jalapeño peppers

*Queso blanco is white Mexican cheese. It is available in most large supermarkets and in Mexican markets.

1. Heat oil in large skillet over medium-high heat. Add chicken; cook and stir until cooked through. Remove from skillet; set aside.

2. Add onion to skillet; cook and stir until translucent. Add tomatoes, chili powder, cumin, salt, garlic powder, oregano and coriander. Cook and stir 15 minutes or until thickened. Add chicken; mix well.

3. Preheat oven to 450°F. Divide chicken mixture among tortillas; roll up tightly. Place, seam side down, in 13×9-inch baking dish. Bake 15 minutes or until tortillas are crisp and brown. Sprinkle with queso blanco; bake 5 minutes or until cheese is melted. Sprinkle with cilantro. Serve with salsa and jalapeños.

Makes 4 to 5 servings

Mole Chicken

3 tablespoons vegetable oil
1 cut-up whole chicken (4 pounds)
1 medium onion, chopped
1 green bell pepper, diced
3 cloves garlic, chopped
2 tablespoons chili powder
2 teaspoons ground cumin
½ teaspoon ground cinnamon
1 can (about 14 ounces) diced tomatoes
1 cup *each* chicken broth and dark Mexican beer
¼ cup raisins
2 chipotle peppers in adobo sauce, chopped
2 tablespoons peanut butter
1 tablespoon sugar
1 teaspoon salt
2 squares (1 ounce each) unsweetened chocolate, chopped
Hot cooked rice and black beans (optional)

1. Heat oil in large skillet over medium heat. Add chicken in batches; brown on all sides. Place in large baking pan; set aside.

2. Add onion, bell pepper and garlic to skillet; cook and stir 5 minutes or until vegetables are softened. Stir in chili powder, cumin and cinnamon; cook 5 minutes. Add tomatoes, broth, beer, raisins, chipotles, peanut butter, sugar and salt; bring to a simmer. Cook 20 minutes, stirring often. Place vegetable mixture and chocolate in food processor or blender; process until smooth.

3. Preheat oven to 350°F. Pour sauce over chicken. Cover pan loosely with foil; bake 45 minutes or until chicken is cooked through (165°F) and sauce is bubbly. Serve with rice and beans, if desired. *Makes 4 servings*

Chicken Fiesta

Chicken Fajitas

1 pound chicken tenders
¼ cup fresh lime juice
4 cloves garlic, minced and divided
  Nonstick cooking spray
1 cup *each* sliced red, green and yellow bell peppers
¾ cup onion slices (about 1 medium)
½ teaspoon ground cumin
¼ teaspoon salt
¼ teaspoon ground red pepper
3 tablespoons sour cream
8 (6-inch) flour tortillas, warmed
  Green onion tops (optional)
  Rice and beans (optional)

1. Arrange chicken in 11×7-inch glass baking dish. Add lime juice and half of garlic; toss to coat. Cover; marinate in refrigerator 30 minutes, stirring occasionally.

2. Spray large nonstick skillet with cooking spray; heat over medium heat. Add chicken mixture; cook and stir 5 to 7 minutes or until browned and no longer pink in center. Remove chicken from skillet; drain excess liquid from skillet.

3. Add bell peppers, onion and remaining garlic to skillet; cook and stir about 5 minutes or until tender. Sprinkle with cumin, salt and ground red pepper. Return chicken to skillet; cook and stir 1 to 2 minutes.

4. Spread sour cream evenly on one side of each tortilla. Spoon chicken and bell pepper mixture over sour cream; roll up tortillas. Tie each tortilla with green onion top and serve with rice and beans, if desired.

Makes 4 servings

Chicken Fiesta

Chicken and Bean Tostadas

Nonstick cooking spray
¾ pound boneless skinless chicken breasts, cut into ¾-inch pieces
1 yellow, green or red bell pepper, diced
1 cup chopped yellow onion
2 teaspoons ground cumin
1 cup chunky salsa, divided
1 can (about 15 ounces) refried beans
8 tostada shells
¼ cup chopped fresh cilantro or green onion

1. Coat large nonstick skillet with cooking spray; heat over medium heat. Add chicken, bell pepper, onion and cumin; cook, stirring occasionally, 6 minutes or until chicken is no longer pink. Stir in ¾ cup salsa. Reduce heat; simmer 5 to 6 minutes or until chicken is cooked through.

2. Meanwhile, combine beans with remaining ¼ cup salsa in microwavable bowl. Microwave on HIGH 3 minutes or until heated through, stirring occasionally. Spread mixture over tostada shells. Top with chicken mixture and cilantro.

Makes 4 servings

TIP

Offer a variety of toppings with tostadas, such as fresh tomatoes, shredded lettuce, cheese, sour cream and guacamole.

Chicken Fiesta

Chipotle Chicken Taquitos

2 cups shredded cooked chicken*

¾ cup water

½ cup ORTEGA® Thick & Chunky Salsa

1 packet (1.25 ounces) ORTEGA® Chipotle Taco Seasoning Mix

1 cup vegetable oil, for frying

8 (8-inch) ORTEGA® Soft Flour Tortillas

1 can (16 ounces) ORTEGA® Refried Beans

1 cup (4 ounces) shredded Cheddar cheese

Sour cream

Additional ORTEGA® Thick & Chunky Salsa

*Purchase a cooked rotisserie chicken at the supermarket deli department.

Combine chicken, water, salsa and seasoning mix in medium skillet over low heat. Cook and stir until well combined. Transfer mixture to medium bowl. Clean skillet. Line platter with paper towels.

Heat oil in skillet over medium-high heat. Meanwhile, wrap tortillas with clean, lightly moistened cloth or paper towels. Microwave on HIGH (100% power) 1 minute, or until hot and pliable.

Divide beans evenly among tortillas, spreading down center of each tortilla. Top with 2 tablespoons chicken mixture. Sprinkle cheese evenly over chicken mixture.

Roll each tortilla tightly. Carefully place in hot oil, seam side down. Cook about 3 minutes. Turn over and continue cooking until golden brown. Drain on paper towels and repeat with remaining tortillas. Serve with sour cream and salsa. *Makes 4 servings*

Prep Time: 10 minutes
Start to Finish: 30 minutes

Chicken & Spinach Quesadillas with Pico de Gallo

  2 cups chopped seeded tomatoes (2 medium), divided
  1 cup chopped green onions, divided
  ½ cup minced fresh cilantro
  1 tablespoon minced jalapeño pepper
  1 tablespoon fresh lime juice
  1 cup packed chopped stemmed spinach
  1 cup shredded cooked boneless skinless chicken breast
 10 (8-inch) flour tortillas
  ¾ cup (3 ounces) shredded Cheddar cheese
    Nonstick cooking spray

1. For pico de gallo, combine 1½ cups tomatoes, ¾ cup green onions, cilantro, jalapeño and lime juice in medium bowl; set aside.

2. Divide remaining ½ cup tomatoes, ¼ cup green onions, spinach and chicken among 5 tortillas; sprinkle with cheese. Top with remaining 5 tortillas.

3. Spray large nonstick skillet with cooking spray. Cook quesadillas, 1 at a time, over medium heat 2 minutes per side or until lightly browned and cheese is melted. Cut each quesadilla into 4 wedges and serve with pico de gallo.   *Makes 5 servings*

Grilled Chicken with Corn and Black Bean Salsa

½ cup corn
½ cup finely chopped red bell pepper
½ (15-ounce) can black beans, rinsed and drained
½ ripe medium avocado, diced
¼ cup chopped fresh cilantro
 2 tablespoons fresh lime juice
 1 tablespoon chopped sliced pickled jalapeño pepper
½ teaspoon salt, divided
 1 teaspoon black pepper
½ teaspoon chili powder
 4 boneless skinless chicken breasts, pounded to ½-inch thickness
   Nonstick cooking spray

1. Combine corn, bell pepper, beans, avocado, cilantro, lime juice, jalapeño and ¼ teaspoon salt in medium bowl. Set aside.

2. Combine black pepper, chili powder and remaining ¼ teaspoon salt in small bowl; sprinkle over chicken.

3. Coat grill pan with cooking spray. Cook chicken over medium-high heat 4 minutes per side or until no longer pink in center.

4. Serve chicken with salsa.

Makes 4 servings

Chicken Fiesta

Creamy Enchiladas Verde

1 can (10¾ ounces) CAMPBELL'S® Condensed Creamy
    Chicken Verde Soup
½ teaspoon garlic powder
1½ cups chopped cooked chicken
⅔ cup shredded Cheddar or Monterey Jack cheese
8 corn tortillas (6-inch), warmed
¼ cup milk

1. Mix ½ can of the soup, garlic powder, chicken and ⅓ cup cheese in a medium bowl.

2. Spoon about ⅓ cup of the chicken mixture down the center of each tortilla. Roll up the tortillas and place them seam-side down in a 12×8×2-inch shallow baking dish.

3. Stir the remaining soup and milk in a small bowl and pour over the filled tortillas. Top with the remaining cheese.

4. Bake at 375°F. for 20 minutes or until the enchiladas are hot and bubbly.
Makes 4 servings

Prep Time: 10 minutes
Bake Time: 20 minutes

Menu

Grilled Baja Burritos

Spicy Margarita Shrimp

Fillets with Mole Verde

Beer and Chipotle Fish Tacos

Chilean Sea Bass Veracruz

Shrimp Tostadas

Baked Fish Steaks

Spicy Tuna Empanadas

Seafood Veracruz

Tuna Quesadilla Stacks

Fish & Shellfish

Grilled Baja Burritos

1 pound tilapia, halibut or snapper fillets

6 tablespoons vegetable oil, divided

3 tablespoons fresh lime juice, divided

2 teaspoons chili powder

1½ teaspoons lemon pepper

3 cups coleslaw mix

½ cup chopped fresh cilantro

¼ teaspoon salt

¼ teaspoon black pepper

Guacamole

Pico de gallo

4 (7-inch) flour tortillas

Lime wedges (optional)

1. Prepare grill for direct cooking or preheat broiler to medium-high heat (400°F). Place fish, 2 tablespoons oil, 1 tablespoon lime juice, chili powder and lemon pepper in large resealable food storage bag. Turn to coat; let stand 10 minutes.

2. Brush grid with 2 tablespoons oil. Remove fish from marinade; discard marinade. Grill fish over medium-high heat, covered, 6 to 8 minutes or until center is opaque, carefully turning once. (To broil, place 4 inches away from heat source. Broil 3 to 5 minutes per side or until center is opaque.)

3. Combine coleslaw mix, cilantro, remaining 2 tablespoons oil, remaining 2 tablespoons lime juice, salt and black pepper in medium bowl.

4. Layer fish, coleslaw mixture, guacamole and pico de gallo on bottom of tortillas. Tightly roll up bottom and sides of tortillas. Cut in half on an angle to serve. Serve with additional pico de gallo and lime wedges, if desired.

Makes 4 servings

Spicy Margarita Shrimp

⅔ cup *Frank's® RedHot®* Original Cayenne Pepper Sauce

¼ cup olive oil

2 tablespoons lime juice

1 teaspoon grated lime zest

2 teaspoons minced garlic

1½ pounds jumbo shrimp, shelled and deveined

1 (16-ounce) jar mild chunky salsa

2 tablespoons minced cilantro

2 red or orange bell peppers, cut into chunks

1. Whisk together *Frank's RedHot* Sauce, oil, lime juice, zest and garlic. Place shrimp into resealable plastic bag. Pour ⅔ cup marinade over shrimp. Seal bag; marinate in refrigerator 30 minutes.

2. Combine remaining marinade with salsa and cilantro in bowl; set aside.

3. Place shrimp and bell pepper chunks on metal skewers. Grill over medium-high direct heat about 8 minutes until shrimp turn pink. Serve with spicy salsa on the side. *Makes 4 to 6 servings*

Prep Time: 10 minutes
Cook Time: 8 minutes
Marinate Time: 30 minutes

Variation: To make Mesa Grill BBQ Sauce, add ½ cup *Frank's® RedHot®* Original Cayenne Pepper Sauce to 1 cup *Cattlemen's®* Authentic Smoke House Barbecue Sauce.

Fillets with Mole Verde

4 tablespoons vegetable oil, divided

¼ cup chopped white onion

1 to 2 jalapeño peppers, seeded and finely chopped

1 cup tomatillos, husked and chopped *or* 1 can (8 ounces) tomatillos, drained and chopped

2 cloves garlic, minced

¼ teaspoon ground cumin

⅓ cup plus 1 tablespoon water, divided

⅓ cup coarsely chopped fresh cilantro

½ teaspoon salt, divided

⅓ cup all-purpose flour

⅛ teaspoon black pepper

1 egg

2 tablespoons butter

1½ to 2 pounds small red snapper fillets or skinless sole fillets

1. Heat 2 tablespoons oil in medium skillet over medium heat. Add onion and jalapeños; cook and stir 4 minutes or until softened. Add tomatillos, garlic and cumin; cook and stir 1 minute.

2. Add ⅓ cup water, cilantro and ¼ teaspoon salt; bring to a boil over high heat. Reduce heat to low; cover and simmer 20 minutes. Transfer to food processor or blender; process until smooth. Return sauce to skillet. Set aside.

3. Combine flour, remaining ¼ teaspoon salt and black pepper in shallow dish. Beat egg with remaining 1 tablespoon water in shallow bowl.

4. Heat butter and remaining 2 tablespoons oil in 12-inch skillet over medium-high heat until foamy. Working with as many fillets as will fit in

continued on page 110

Fillets with Mole Verde, continued

skillet in single layer, lightly coat fillets on both sides with flour mixture; shake off excess. Dip into egg mixture; let excess drain off. Cook 4 to 8 minutes or until light brown on outside and opaque in center, turning once. Remove to serving plate; keep warm. Repeat with remaining fillets.

5. Heat reserved sauce over medium heat, stirring frequently. Pour over fish.

Makes 4 to 6 servings

Beer and Chipotle Fish Tacos

1½ pounds cod, grouper or other white fish fillets, cut into thin strips
1 bottle (12 ounces) light-colored beer, such as pale ale
½ cup yellow cornmeal
1 teaspoon chipotle chili powder
½ teaspoon salt
2 tablespoons olive oil
8 (6-inch) corn tortillas, warmed
1½ cups shredded cabbage
   Lime juice
   Chopped fresh tomatoes and chopped fresh cilantro

1. Place fish in shallow dish. Pour beer over fish; marinate 15 to 30 minutes.

2. Combine cornmeal, chipotle chili powder and salt in another shallow dish. Drain fish; dredge in cornmeal mixture.

3. Heat oil in large skillet over medium-high heat. Cook fish 3 to 4 minutes on each side or until fish begins to flake when tested with fork.

4. Serve fish in tortillas with cabbage. Drizzle with lime juice; top with tomatoes and cilantro.

Makes 6 to 8 servings

Chilean Sea Bass Veracruz

¾ **pound Chilean sea bass steaks or halibut steaks, skinned, boned and cut into 1-inch cubes**

3 **tablespoons fresh lime juice, divided**

⅛ **teaspoon black pepper**

4 **large tomatoes, seeded and diced**

1 **large onion, diced**

3 **cloves garlic, minced**

2 **to 3 serrano peppers, seeded and finely chopped**

Olive oil cooking spray

2 **tablespoons chopped fresh cilantro**

3 **cups hot cooked rice**

1. Place fish, 1 tablespoon lime juice and black pepper in small bowl. Stir well and let marinate at least 15 minutes, but not more than 30 minutes.

2. Meanwhile, combine tomatoes, onion and garlic in medium bowl. Stir in serrano peppers; mix well.

3. Spray large nonstick skillet with cooking spray; heat over high heat. Add fish; cook and stir 2 to 3 minutes or until lightly browned. Reduce heat to medium; cook and stir about 5 minutes or until fish begins to flake when tested with fork. Remove fish to clean bowl; set aside.

4. Add tomato mixture to skillet; cook and stir about 3 minutes or just until onions are soft. Return fish to skillet; cook and stir 2 minutes. Remove from heat. Add remaining 2 tablespoons lime juice and cilantro. Serve over rice.

Makes 4 servings

Shrimp Tostadas

1 pound cooked shrimp, peeled, deveined
1 can (14.5 ounces) diced tomatoes, drained
1 cup chopped white onion
1 can (4 ounces) ORTEGA® Fire-Roasted Diced Green Chiles
¼ cup chopped fresh cilantro
3 tablespoons vegetable oil
3 tablespoons lime juice
1 can (16 ounces) ORTEGA® Refried Beans, warmed
1 package (10-count) ORTEGA® Tostada Shells, warmed
2½ cups shredded lettuce

Combine shrimp, tomatoes, onions, chiles, cilantro, oil and lime juice in medium bowl; cover.

Spread about 2 tablespoons beans on each tostada shell. Top with ¼ cup lettuce and ½ cup shrimp mixture.   *Makes 10 servings*

Prep Time: 5 minutes
Start to Finish: 15 minutes

TIP

The shrimp mixture may be prepared in advance, covered and refrigerated.

Baked Fish Steaks

1 tablespoon annatto seeds

1 cup boiling water

1 tablespoon plus 1½ teaspoons orange juice

1 tablespoon plus 1½ teaspoons cider vinegar

2 cloves garlic, chopped

1 small dried de arbol chile, coarsely crumbled

¾ teaspoon ground cumin

½ teaspoon ground allspice

¼ teaspoon salt

⅛ teaspoon black pepper

4 halibut steaks, mackerel fillets or sea bass fillets
  (about 8 ounces each)

1. Place annatto seeds in small bowl; cover with boiling water. Let stand, covered, at room temperature 8 hours or overnight.

2. Drain annatto seeds; discard liquid. Place annatto seeds, orange juice, vinegar, garlic, chile, cumin, allspice, salt and pepper in food processor or blender; process until smooth.

3. Spread annatto paste over both sides of fish to coat. Arrange fish in single layer in well-oiled baking dish. Cover and refrigerate 1 to 2 hours to allow flavors to blend.

4. Preheat oven to 350°F. Bake fish, uncovered, 20 to 25 minutes or until fish begins to flake when tested with fork.   *Makes 4 servings*

Spicy Tuna Empanadas

2 (2.6-ounce) STARKIST Flavor Fresh Pouch® Tuna
   (Albacore or Chunk Light)
1 can (4 ounces) diced green chilies, drained
1 can (2¼ ounces) sliced ripe olives, drained
½ cup shredded sharp Cheddar cheese
1 chopped hard-cooked egg
   Salt and pepper to taste
¼ teaspoon hot pepper sauce
¼ cup medium thick and chunky salsa
2 packages (15 ounces each) refrigerated pie crusts
   Additional salsa

In medium bowl, place tuna, chilies, olives, cheese, egg, salt, pepper and hot pepper sauce; toss lightly with fork. Add ¼ cup salsa and toss again; set aside. Following directions on package, unfold pie crusts (roll out slightly with rolling pin if you prefer thinner crust); cut 4 circles, 4 inches each, out of each crust. Place 8 circles on foil-covered baking sheets; wet edge of each circle with water. Top each circle with ¼ cup lightly packed tuna mixture. Top with remaining circles, stretching pastry slightly to fit; press edges together and crimp with fork. Cut slits in top crust to vent. Bake in 425°F oven 15 to 18 minutes or until golden brown. Cool slightly. Serve with additional salsa.

Makes 8 servings

Seafood Veracruz

1 can (8 ounces) HUNT'S® Tomato Sauce
½ cup chunky tomato pico de gallo or salsa
1 pound fresh cod or whitefish fillets

1. Preheat oven to 450°F.

2. Combine tomato sauce and pico de gallo in small bowl.

3. Divide fish fillets on 4 individual sheets of foil; top with tomato mixture. Seal foil to form packets.

4. Bake on cookie sheet 20 minutes.   *Makes 4 servings*

Hands On: 10 minutes
Total Time: 30 minutes

TIP

Pico de gallo is a traditional salsa that consists of chopped fresh ingredients such as tomatoes, oranges, jicama, bell peppers, onions and jalapeño peppers.

Tuna Quesadilla Stacks

4 (10-inch) flour tortillas

¼ cup plus 2 tablespoons pinto or black bean dip

1 can (about 14 ounces) diced tomatoes, drained

1 can (9 ounces) tuna packed in water, drained and flaked

2 cups (8 ounces) shredded Cheddar cheese

½ cup thinly sliced green onions

1½ teaspoons butter, melted

1. Preheat oven to 400°F.

2. Place 1 tortilla on 12-inch pizza pan. Spread with 2 tablespoons bean dip, leaving ½-inch border. Top with one third each of tomatoes, tuna, cheese and green onions. Repeat layers twice, beginning with tortilla and ending with green onions.

3. Top with remaining tortilla, pressing gently. Brush with melted butter.

4. Bake 15 minutes or until cheese melts and top is lightly browned. Cool slightly. Cut into 8 wedges.   *Makes 4 servings*

Prep and Cook Time: 25 minutes

MENU

- ✳ Four-Pepper Black Bean Fajitas
- ✳ Bean and Vegetable Burritos
- ✳ Veggie-Pepper Bowls with Rice
- ✳ Chile Cheese Puff
- ✳ Black Bean Flautas with Charred Tomatillo Salsa
- ✳ Spicy Vegetable Quesadillas
- ✳ Mexican Tortilla Stack-Ups
- ✳ Black Bean Cakes
- ✳ Spinach and Mushroom Enchiladas
- ✳ Crispy Tostadas
- ✳ Cheesy Stuffed Poblano Peppers

Vegetarian Delights

Four-Pepper Black Bean Fajitas

1 can (about 15 ounces) black beans, rinsed and drained
¼ cup water
3 tablespoons olive oil, divided
2 tablespoons lime juice
1 canned chipotle pepper in adobo sauce
1 clove garlic, minced
¼ teaspoon salt
1 medium red bell pepper, cut into strips
1 medium green bell pepper, cut into strips
1 medium yellow bell pepper, cut into strips
2 medium onions, cut into ¼-inch wedges
8 (8-inch) flour tortillas
¼ cup chopped fresh cilantro
½ cup sour cream
1 medium lime, cut into 8 wedges

1. Combine beans, water, 2 tablespoons oil, lime juice, chipotle, garlic and salt in food processor or blender; process until smooth. Place in medium microwavable bowl. Cover with plastic wrap; set aside.

2. Heat remaining 1 tablespoon oil in large skillet over medium-high heat. Add bell peppers and onions; cook and stir 12 minutes or until beginning to brown.

3. Heat bean mixture in microwave on HIGH 2 to 3 minutes or until heated through. Heat tortillas according to package directions.

4. To serve, divide bean mixture among tortillas; top with bell pepper mixture. Sprinkle with cilantro and serve with sour cream and lime wedges.

Makes 4 servings

Bean and Vegetable Burritos

1 tablespoon olive oil

1 medium onion, thinly sliced

1 jalapeño pepper, seeded and minced

1 tablespoon chili powder

3 cloves garlic, minced

2 teaspoons dried oregano

1 teaspoon ground cumin

1 tablespoon water

1 large sweet potato, baked, cooled, peeled and diced *or* 1 can
 (16 ounces) yams in syrup, rinsed, drained and diced

1 can (about 15 ounces) black beans or pinto beans, rinsed and
 drained

1 cup frozen corn, thawed and drained

1 green bell pepper, chopped

2 tablespoons fresh lime juice

½ cup (2 ounces) shredded Monterey Jack cheese

4 (10-inch) flour tortillas

 Sour cream (optional)

1. Preheat oven to 350°F. Heat oil in large saucepan or Dutch oven over medium-high heat. Add onion; cook and stir 10 minutes or until golden. Add jalapeño, chili powder, garlic, oregano and cumin; cook and stir 1 minute. Stir in water; remove from heat. Stir in potato, beans, corn, bell pepper and lime juice.

2. Spoon 2 tablespoons cheese in center of each tortilla. Top with 1 cup filling. Fold all 4 sides around filling to enclose. Place burritos, seam side down, on baking sheet. Cover with foil and bake 30 minutes or until heated through. Top with sour cream, if desired.   *Makes 4 servings*

Veggie-Pepper Bowls with Rice

8 medium green bell peppers, halved and seeded

3 cups cooked long-grain white rice

1 package (10 ounces) frozen peas and carrots

1 cup whole-kernel corn

½ cup chopped green onions

1¾ cups ORTEGA® Salsa, any variety, divided

1½ cups Mexican-blend cheese, divided

Preheat oven to 375°F.

Place bell peppers in microwave-safe dish with 3 tablespoons water. Cover with plastic wrap. Microwave on HIGH (100%) for 4 to 5 minutes or until slightly tender. Drain.

Combine rice, peas and carrots, corn, green onions, ¾ cup salsa and 1 cup cheese in large bowl. Fill each pepper with about ½ cup rice mixture. Place peppers in ungreased 13×9-inch baking dish; top with remaining salsa and cheese.

Bake, covered, for 20 to 25 minutes. Uncover; bake for additional 5 minutes or until heated through and cheese is melted.

Makes 8 servings

Chile Cheese Puff

¾ cup all-purpose flour

1½ teaspoons baking powder

9 eggs

4 cups (16 ounces) shredded Monterey Jack cheese

2 cups (16 ounces) cottage cheese

2 cans (4 ounces each) diced green chiles, drained

1½ teaspoons sugar

¼ teaspoon salt

⅛ teaspoon hot pepper sauce

1 cup salsa

1. Preheat oven to 350°F. Spray 13×9-inch baking dish with nonstick cooking spray. Combine flour and baking powder in small bowl.

2. Whisk eggs in large bowl until blended; stir in Monterey Jack, cottage cheese, chiles, sugar, salt and hot pepper sauce. Add flour mixture; stir just until blended. Pour into prepared dish.

3. Bake, uncovered, 45 minutes or until set. Let stand 5 minutes before serving. Top with salsa.

Makes 8 servings

Black Bean Flautas with Charred Tomatillo Salsa

Salsa

- 1 pound tomatillos, unpeeled
- 1 small yellow onion, unpeeled
- 6 cloves garlic, unpeeled
- 1 jalapeño pepper
  Juice of ½ lime
  Salt and black pepper

Flautas

- 1 can (about 15 ounces) black beans, undrained
- 1 cup vegetable broth
- 1 teaspoon salt, divided
- ½ teaspoon ground cumin
- ½ teaspoon chili powder
- 3 cloves garlic, minced
- ¼ cup chopped fresh cilantro
  Juice of 1 lime
- 10 (6-inch) flour tortillas
- 2½ cups (10 ounces) shredded Colby Jack cheese
- 1 cup seeded and chopped tomatoes (about 2 tomatoes)
- 1 cup thinly sliced green onions

1. For salsa, cook and stir tomatillos, onion, garlic and jalapeño in dry large heavy skillet over medium-high heat about 20 minutes or until soft and skins are blackened. Remove from skillet; cool 5 minutes. Peel tomatillos, onion and garlic; remove stem and seeds from jalapeño. Place tomatillo

continued on page 134

Black Bean Flautas with Charred Tomatillo Salsa, *continued*

mixture and lime juice in blender or food processor; blend until smooth. Season to taste with salt and pepper. Set aside.

2. For flautas, place beans and liquid, broth, ½ teaspoon salt, cumin, chili powder and garlic in medium saucepan. Bring to a boil over medium-high heat. Reduce heat; simmer 10 minutes or until beans are very soft. Drain; reserve liquid. Place drained bean mixture, cilantro, lime juice and remaining ½ teaspoon salt in blender or food processor; purée until smooth. (Add reserved liquid, 1 teaspoon at a time, if beans are dry.)

3. Preheat oven to 450°F. Spread bean purée evenly on each tortilla; sprinkle with cheese, tomatoes and green onions. Roll up tightly and place, seam side down, in 13×9-inch baking dish.

4. Bake 10 to 15 minutes or until crisp and brown and cheese is melted. Serve with salsa. *Makes 5 servings*

TIP

Select solid, firm tomatillos with smooth, unbroken skins and clean husks that are not blackened by mildew or softened by juice. Unlike tomatoes, tomatillos are ready to use while still quite firm. One pound of tomatillos equals 6 to 8 medium.

Spicy Vegetable Quesadillas

Nonstick cooking spray
1 small zucchini, chopped
½ cup chopped onion
½ cup chopped green bell pepper
2 cloves garlic, minced
½ teaspoon chili powder
½ teaspoon ground cumin
8 (6-inch) flour tortillas
1 cup (4 ounces) shredded Cheddar cheese
¼ cup chopped fresh cilantro

1. Spray large nonstick skillet with cooking spray; heat over medium heat. Add zucchini, onion, bell pepper, garlic, chili powder and cumin; cook and stir 3 to 4 minutes or until vegetables are crisp-tender.

2. Spoon vegetable mixture evenly over half of each tortilla. Sprinkle evenly with cheese and cilantro. Fold each tortilla in half.

3. Wipe skillet clean. Spray skillet with cooking spray. Add quesadillas; heat over medium heat 1 to 2 minutes per side or until lightly browned. Cut into thirds before serving.

Makes 8 servings

Vegetarian Delights

Mexican Tortilla Stack-Ups

1 tablespoon vegetable oil

½ cup chopped onion

1 can (about 15 ounces) black beans, rinsed and drained

1 can (about 14 ounces) Mexican-style diced tomatoes

1 cup frozen corn

1 envelope (1¼ ounces) taco seasoning mix

6 (6-inch) corn tortillas

2 cups (8 ounces) shredded taco cheese blend

1 cup water

1. Preheat oven to 350°F. Spray 13×9-inch baking dish with nonstick cooking spray.

2. Heat oil in large skillet over medium-high heat. Add onion; cook and stir 3 minutes or until tender. Add beans, tomatoes, corn and taco seasoning mix; bring to a boil over high heat. Reduce heat to low and simmer 5 minutes.

3. Place 2 tortillas side by side in prepared dish. Top each tortilla with about ½ cup bean mixture. Sprinkle evenly with one third of cheese. Repeat layers twice, creating 2 tortilla stacks each 3 tortillas high.

4. Pour water along sides of tortillas. Cover tightly with foil and bake 30 to 35 minutes or until heated through. Cut into wedges to serve.

Makes 6 servings

Black Bean Cakes

1 can (about 15 ounces) black beans, rinsed and drained
¼ cup all-purpose flour
¼ cup chopped fresh cilantro
2 tablespoons sour cream
1 tablespoon chili powder
2 cloves garlic, minced
1 tablespoon vegetable oil
   Salsa
   Hot cooked rice (optional)

1. Place beans in medium bowl; mash with fork or potato masher until almost smooth, leaving some beans in larger pieces. Stir in flour, cilantro, sour cream, chili powder and garlic. Shape bean mixture into 8 patties.

2. Heat oil in large nonstick skillet over medium-high heat. Cook bean patties 6 to 8 minutes or until lightly browned, turning once. Top with salsa; serve with rice, if desired.   *Makes 4 servings*

TIP

Store fresh cilantro in the refrigerator for up to one week with the stems in a glass of water and the leaves covered with a plastic bag.

Spinach and Mushroom Enchiladas

2 packages (10 ounces each) frozen chopped spinach, thawed and
squeezed dry

1½ cups sliced mushrooms

1 can (about 15 ounces) pinto beans, rinsed and drained

3 teaspoons chili powder, divided

¼ teaspoon red pepper flakes

1 can (about 8 ounces) tomato sauce

2 tablespoons water

½ teaspoon hot pepper sauce

8 (8-inch) corn tortillas

1 cup (4 ounces) shredded Monterey Jack cheese

Shredded lettuce, chopped tomatoes, sour cream and chopped fresh
cilantro (optional)

1. Cook and stir spinach, mushrooms, beans, 2 teaspoons chili powder and
red pepper flakes in large skillet over medium heat 5 minutes. Combine
tomato sauce, water, remaining 1 teaspoon chili powder and hot pepper
sauce in medium skillet.

2. Dip each tortilla into tomato sauce mixture. Spoon spinach filling
evenly onto center of tortillas; roll up and place, seam side down, in
11×8-inch microwavable dish. Secure rolls with toothpicks, if necessary.
Spread remaining tomato sauce mixture over enchiladas.

3. Cover with vented plastic wrap. Microwave on MEDIUM (50%)
10 minutes or until heated through. Sprinkle with cheese. Microwave on
MEDIUM (50%) 3 minutes or until cheese is melted. Serve with lettuce,
tomatoes, sour cream and cilantro, if desired. Remove and discard
toothpicks before serving.

Makes 4 servings

Crispy Tostadas

What You Need

8 tostada shells (5 inch)

1 can (16 ounces) TACO BELL® HOME ORIGINALS® Refried Beans

1 cup finely chopped red and green bell peppers

½ pound (8 ounces) VELVEETA® Pepper Jack Pasteurized Prepared Cheese Product, sliced

1 cup shredded lettuce

½ cup TACO BELL® HOME ORIGINALS® Thick 'N Chunky Salsa

Make It

1. PREHEAT oven to 350°F. Spread tostada shells with beans; top evenly with bell peppers and VELVEETA®.

2. BAKE 5 to 7 minutes or until VELVEETA® is melted.

3. TOP with lettuce and salsa.

Makes 8 servings

Prep Time: 10 minutes
Total Time: 17 minutes

Crispy Tostada

Cheesy Stuffed Poblano Peppers

3 tablespoons olive oil, divided

1 cup frozen corn, thawed

1 cup diced red onion, divided

¾ cup (3 ounces) crumbled queso blanco cheese

½ cup (2 ounces) shredded Monterey Jack cheese

¼ cup minced fresh cilantro

2 teaspoons minced garlic, divided

4 poblano peppers

2 medium tomatoes, seeded and diced

Juice of 1 lime

Salt and black pepper

1. Preheat oven to 450°F. Heat 1 tablespoon oil in small skillet over medium-high heat. Add corn and ½ cup onion; cook and stir 5 minutes. Remove to large bowl. Add cheeses, cilantro and 1 teaspoon garlic; mix well.

2. Make two long slits on front of each poblano to create flap. Lift flap; remove and discard seeds and ribs. Divide corn mixture evenly among poblanos. Replace flap; secure with wooden skewer, if desired. Place stuffed poblanos in baking dish. Brush skins with 1 tablespoon oil.

3. Roast poblanos 15 to 20 minutes or until skins are wrinkled and filling is melted. Meanwhile, combine tomatoes, remaining ½ cup onion, lime juice, remaining 1 tablespoon oil, 1 teaspoon garlic, salt and black pepper in medium bowl. Serve tomato mixture with poblanos. *Makes 4 servings*

Cheesy Stuffed Poblano Pepper

Menu

- Fiesta-Style Roasted Vegetables
- Mexican-Style Corn on the Cob
- Veg•All® Refried Beans
- Mexican Slaw
- Green Chile Rice
- Zesty Pico de Gallo
- Confetti Black Beans
- Crunchy Mexican Side Salad
- Guacamole
- Arroz Rojos
- Charred Corn Salad

Side Orders

Fiesta-Style Roasted Vegetables

1 can (4 ounces) ORTEGA® Fire-Roasted Diced Green Chiles

3 tablespoons vinegar

2 tablespoons vegetable oil

1 packet (1.25 ounces) ORTEGA® Taco Seasoning Mix

1 small red bell pepper, cut into strips

1 medium zucchini, cut into ½-inch slices

1 small sweet potato, peeled, halved and cut into ⅛-inch slices

1 small red onion, cut into wedges

Nonstick cooking spray

Combine chiles, vinegar, oil and seasoning mix in large bowl; mix well. Add red pepper, zucchini, sweet potato and onion; toss gently to coat. Let stand at room temperature 15 minutes to marinate.

Preheat oven to 450°F. Cover 15×10-inch baking pan with foil and spray with cooking spray.

Remove vegetables from marinade with spoon; place on prepared pan.

Bake 20 to 25 minutes until tender and browned, stirring once.

Makes 4 servings

Variation: Substitute yellow squash for the zucchini, if preferred.

Mexican-Style Corn on the Cob

    2 tablespoons mayonnaise
    ½ teaspoon chili powder
    ½ teaspoon grated lime peel
    4 ears corn, shucked
    2 tablespoons grated Parmesan cheese

1. Prepare grill for direct cooking. Combine mayonnaise, chili powder and lime peel in small bowl; set aside.

2. Grill corn over medium-high heat, uncovered, 4 to 6 minutes or until lightly charred, turning 3 times. Immediately spread mayonnaise mixture over corn. Sprinkle with cheese.   *Makes 4 servings*

Veg•All® Refried Beans

    1 can (4.5 ounces) chopped green chilies, undrained
    1 can (15 ounces) VEG•ALL® Original Mixed Vegetables, drained
    1 can (15 ounces) ALLENS® or TRAPPEY'S® pinto beans, undrained
    1 tablespoon fresh lime juice
      Salt and pepper to taste
    1 can (2.25 ounces) sliced black olives, drained
    ½ cup shredded Cheddar cheese

Preheat oven to 350°F.

In a medium mixing bowl, mash chilies, Veg•All and pinto beans. Sauté in oil until very thick (10 to 15 minutes). Add lime juice, salt and pepper.

Spoon vegetable mixture into a small casserole dish or pie pan.

Top with black olives and cheese. Bake for 10 to 15 minutes or until cheese is melted and bubbling.   *Makes 6 to 8 servings*

Mexican Slaw

1 (6-inch) corn tortilla, cut into thin strips
   Nonstick cooking spray
¼ teaspoon chili powder
3 cups shredded green cabbage
1 cup shredded red cabbage
½ cup shredded carrots
½ cup sliced radishes
½ cup corn
¼ cup coarsely chopped fresh cilantro
¼ cup mayonnaise
1 tablespoon fresh lime juice
2 teaspoons cider vinegar
1 teaspoon honey
½ teaspoon ground cumin
   Salt and black pepper

1. Preheat oven to 350°F. Arrange tortilla strips in even layer on nonstick baking sheet. Spray strips with cooking spray and sprinkle with chili powder. Bake 6 to 8 minutes or until crisp.

2. Combine cabbage, carrots, radishes, corn and cilantro in large bowl. Combine mayonnaise, lime juice, vinegar, honey, cumin, salt and pepper in small bowl. Add mayonnaise mixture to cabbage mixture; toss gently to coat. Top with baked tortilla strips. *Makes 8 servings*

Green Chile Rice

1 cup uncooked white rice
1 can (about 14 ounces) chicken broth plus water to measure 2 cups
1 can (4 ounces) diced mild green chiles
½ medium yellow onion, diced
1 teaspoon dried oregano
½ teaspoon salt
½ teaspoon cumin seeds
3 green onions, thinly sliced
⅓ to ½ cup chopped fresh cilantro

1. Combine rice, broth, chiles, onion, oregano, salt and cumin in large saucepan. Bring to a boil over high heat.

2. Reduce heat to low; cover and simmer 18 minutes or until liquid is absorbed and rice is tender. Stir in green onions and cilantro.

Makes 6 servings

Zesty Pico de Gallo

2 cups chopped seeded tomatoes
1 cup chopped green onions
1 can (about 8 ounces) tomato sauce
½ cup minced fresh cilantro
1 to 2 tablespoons minced jalapeño peppers
1 tablespoon fresh lime juice

1. Combine tomatoes, green onions, tomato sauce, cilantro, jalapeños and lime juice in medium bowl. Cover and refrigerate at least 1 hour.

Makes about 4 cups

Confetti Black Beans

1 cup dried black beans

3 cups water

1 can (about 14 ounces) chicken broth

1 bay leaf

1½ teaspoons olive oil

1 medium onion, chopped

¼ cup chopped red bell pepper

¼ cup chopped yellow bell pepper

2 cloves garlic, minced

1 jalapeño pepper, finely chopped

1 large tomato, seeded and chopped

½ teaspoon salt

⅛ teaspoon black pepper

Hot pepper sauce (optional)

1. Sort and rinse beans; cover with water. Soak 8 hours or overnight. Drain.

2. Place beans and broth in large saucepan; bring to a boil over high heat. Add bay leaf. Reduce heat to low; cover and simmer about 1½ hours or until beans are tender.

3. Heat oil in large skillet over medium heat. Add onion, bell peppers, garlic and jalapeño; cook and stir 8 to 10 minutes or until onion is tender. Add tomato, salt and black pepper; cook 5 minutes.

4. Add onion mixture to beans; cook 15 to 20 minutes. Remove bay leaf before serving. Serve with hot pepper sauce, if desired.   *Makes 6 servings*

Crunchy Mexican Side Salad

3 cups romaine and iceberg lettuce blend

½ cup grape tomatoes, halved

½ cup peeled and diced jicama

¼ cup B&G® Sliced Ripe Olives

¼ cup ORTEGA® Sliced Jalapeños, quartered

2 tablespoons ORTEGA® Taco Sauce

1 tablespoon vegetable oil

⅛ teaspoon salt

Crushed ORTEGA® Taco Shells (optional)

Toss together lettuce, tomatoes, jicama, olives and jalapeños in large bowl.

Combine taco sauce, oil and salt in small bowl. Stir with a fork until blended.

Pour dressing over salad; toss gently to coat. Top with taco shells, if desired. *Makes 4 servings (1 cup each)*

Note: ORTEGA® Sliced Jalapeños are available in a 12-ounce jar. They are pickled, adding great flavor and crunch to this salad.

Guacamole

2 large avocados

¼ cup finely chopped tomato

2 tablespoons fresh lime juice or lemon juice

2 tablespoons grated onion with juice

½ teaspoon salt

¼ teaspoon hot pepper sauce

Black pepper

1. Place avocados in medium bowl; mash coarsely with fork. Stir in tomato, lime juice, onion, salt, hot pepper sauce and black pepper; mix well.

2. Serve immediately or cover and refrigerate up to 2 hours.

Makes 2 cups

Arroz Rojos

  2 tablespoons vegetable oil

  1 cup uncooked long grain white rice (not converted)

  ½ cup finely chopped white onion

  1 clove garlic, minced

  ½ teaspoon salt

  ½ teaspoon ground cumin

    Dash chili powder

  2 large tomatoes, peeled, seeded and chopped

1½ cups chicken broth

  ⅓ cup peas

  2 tablespoons chopped pimiento

1. Heat oil in medium skillet over medium heat. Add rice; cook and stir 2 minutes or until rice turns opaque. Add onion; cook and stir 1 minute. Stir in garlic, salt, cumin and chili powder. Add tomatoes; cook and stir 2 minutes.

2. Stir in broth; bring to a boil over high heat. Reduce heat to low. Cover and simmer 15 minutes or until rice is almost tender. Stir in peas and pimiento. Cover and cook 2 to 4 minutes or until rice is tender and all liquid has been absorbed.

Makes 4 to 6 servings

Charred Corn Salad

   3 tablespoons fresh lime juice

   ½ teaspoon salt

   ¼ cup extra virgin olive oil

   4 to 6 ears corn, shucked (enough to make 3 to 4 cups kernels)

   ⅔ cup canned black beans, rinsed and drained

   ½ cup chopped fresh cilantro

   2 teaspoons minced seeded chipotle pepper*

*You may also use canned chipotle peppers in adobo sauce. They are available in the Mexican food section of most large supermarkets.

1. Whisk lime juice and salt in small bowl. Gradually whisk in oil. Set aside.

2. Heat large skillet over medium-high heat. Cook corn in single layer 15 to 17 minutes or until browned and tender, turning frequently. Transfer to plate to cool slightly. Slice kernels off ears and place in medium bowl.

3. Microwave beans in small microwavable bowl on HIGH 1 minute or until heated through. Add beans, cilantro and chipotle to corn; mix well. Pour lime juice mixture over corn mixture; toss to combine.   *Makes 6 servings*

TIP

To shuck corn, pull outer husks down the ear to the base. Snap off the husks and stem at the base. Strip away the silk from the corn by hand or with a dry vegetable brush. Trim any blemishes from the corn and rinse under cold running water.

MENU

Cinnamon Tacos with Fruit Salsa

Crispy Battered Plantains

Classic Margaritas

Mexican Wedding Cookies

Sangrita

Mango Virgin Margaritas

Pumpkin Flan

Rice Pudding Mexicana

Mexican Coffee with Chocolate & Cinnamon

Deep-Fried Ice Cream

Spanish Churros

Toasted Almond Horchata

Lemon-Lime Watermelon Agua Fresca

Mexican Hot Chocolate with Chili-Dusted Ice Cream

Cajeta y Frutas

Tres Leches Cake

Desserts & Drinks

Desserts & Drinks

Cinnamon Tacos with Fruit Salsa

1 cup sliced fresh strawberries

1 cup cubed fresh pineapple

1 cup cubed peeled kiwi

½ teaspoon ORTEGA® Diced Jalapeños

4 tablespoons plus 1 teaspoon granulated sugar, divided

1 tablespoon ground cinnamon

6 (8-inch) ORTEGA® Soft Flour Tortillas

    Nonstick cooking spray

Stir together strawberries, pineapple, kiwi, jalapeños and 4 teaspoons sugar (adjust to taste, if desired) in large bowl; set aside.

Combine remaining 3 tablespoons sugar and cinnamon in small bowl; set aside.

Coat tortillas lightly on both sides with cooking spray. Heat each tortilla in nonstick skillet over medium heat until slightly puffed and golden brown. Remove from heat; immediately dust both sides with cinnamon-sugar mixture. Shake excess cinnamon-sugar back into bowl. Repeat cooking and dusting process until all tortillas are warmed.

Fold tortillas in half and fill with fruit mixture. Serve immediately.

Makes 6 servings

Prep Time: 20 minutes
Start to Finish: 30 minutes

Desserts & Drinks

Classic Margaritas

Lime slices and coarse salt
Ice
4 ounces tequila
2 ounces triple sec
2 ounces lime or lemon juice

1. Rub rim of margarita glasses with lime slices; dip in salt.

2. Fill cocktail shaker half full with ice; add tequila, triple sec and lime juice. Shake until blended; strain into glasses. Garnish with lime slices.

Makes 2 servings

Frozen Margaritas: Rub rim of margarita glasses with lime slices; dip in salt. Combine tequila, triple sec, lime juice and 2 cups ice in blender; blend until smooth. Pour into glasses. Garnish with lime slices. Makes 2 servings.

Frozen Strawberry Margaritas: Rub rim of margarita glasses with lime slices; dip in salt. Combine tequila, triple sec, lime juice, 1 cup frozen strawberries and 1 cup ice in blender; blend until smooth. Pour into glasses. Garnish with lime slices and strawberries. Makes 2 servings.

Sangrita

3 cups DEL MONTE® Tomato Juice
1½ cups orange juice
½ cup salsa
Juice of 1 medium lime

1. Mix all ingredients in large pitcher; chill.

2. Serve over ice with fruit garnishes, if desired.

Makes 6 servings

Prep Time: 3 minutes

Pumpkin Flan

1 can (15 ounces) solid-pack pumpkin

1 can (12 ounces) evaporated milk

1⅔ cups granulated sugar, divided

3 eggs

2 teaspoons vanilla, divided

1 teaspoon ground cinnamon

½ teaspoon ground ginger

½ teaspoon ground nutmeg

½ teaspoon ground cloves

¼ cup whipping cream

1 tablespoon powdered sugar

1. Preheat oven to 300°F. Beat pumpkin, evaporated milk, ⅓ cup granulated sugar, eggs, 1 teaspoon vanilla, cinnamon, ginger, nutmeg and cloves in large bowl with electric mixer at medium speed until blended.

2. Place remaining 1⅓ cups granulated sugar in large saucepan over medium-high heat; cook until melted and golden brown. (Mixture will be very hot.) Carefully pour sugar into 8 (4-ounce) ramekins. Fill each ramekin with pumpkin mixture; place in 15×11-inch baking dish. Pour hot water into dish until halfway up sides of ramekins.

3. Bake 45 to 55 minutes or until knife inserted into centers comes out clean. Let cool. Run knife around edges of ramekins to loosen flans. Invert onto serving plates.

4. Beat whipping cream, powdered sugar and remaining 1 teaspoon vanilla in small bowl with electric mixer at high speed until soft peaks form; spoon onto flans.

Makes 8 servings

Variation: The flan can also be baked in a 9-inch pie pan for 60 minutes.

Mexican Coffee
with Chocolate & Cinnamon

   6 cups water
½ cup ground dark roast coffee
   2 cinnamon sticks
   1 cup half-and-half
⅓ cup chocolate syrup
¼ cup packed dark brown sugar
1½ teaspoons vanilla, divided
   1 cup whipping cream
¼ cup powdered sugar
   Ground cinnamon

1. Place water in drip coffee maker. Place coffee and cinnamon sticks in coffee filter. Combine half-and-half, chocolate syrup, brown sugar and 1 teaspoon vanilla in coffee pot. Place coffee pot with cream mixture in coffee maker. Brew coffee; coffee will drip into chocolate cream mixture.

2. Meanwhile, beat whipping cream in medium bowl with electric mixer at high speed until soft peaks form. Add powdered sugar and remaining ½ teaspoon vanilla; beat until stiff peaks form. Pour coffee into individual coffee cups; top with dollop of whipped cream. Sprinkle with ground cinnamon.

Makes 10 to 12 servings

Desserts & Drinks

Spanish Churros

1 cup water

¼ cup (½ stick) butter

6 tablespoons sugar, divided

¼ teaspoon salt

1 cup all-purpose flour

2 eggs

Vegetable oil for frying

1 teaspoon ground cinnamon

1. Place water, butter, 2 tablespoons sugar and salt in medium saucepan; bring to a boil over high heat. Remove from heat; add flour. Beat with spoon until dough forms ball and releases from side of pan. Vigorously beat in eggs, 1 at a time, until mixture is smooth. Spoon dough into pastry bag fitted with large star tip. Pipe 3×1-inch strips onto waxed paper-lined baking sheet. Freeze 20 minutes.

2. Pour oil into large skillet to ¾-inch depth. Heat oil to 375°F. Transfer frozen dough to hot oil with large spatula, 4 or 5 churros at a time. Fry 3 to 4 minutes or until deep golden brown, turning once. Remove with slotted spoon to paper towels; drain.

3. Combine remaining 4 tablespoons sugar with cinnamon in paper bag. Add warm churros, 1 at a time. Close bag and shake until churros are coated with sugar mixture. Remove to wire rack; cool completely. Store tightly covered at room temperature or freeze up to 3 months.

Makes about 3 dozen churros

Lemon-Lime Watermelon Agua Fresca

10 cups seedless watermelon cubes
 1 cup ice water
 ⅓ cup sugar
 2 tablespoons fresh lemon juice
 2 tablespoons fresh lime juice

1. Combine half of watermelon and water in blender; blend until smooth. Transfer to bowl. Repeat with remaining watermelon and water.

2. Stir in sugar, lemon juice and lime juice; mix until dissolved. Serve immediately over ice or refrigerate until ready to serve.   *Makes 6 servings*

Cajeta y Frutas

 1 can (14 ounces) sweetened condensed milk
 3 cups whipped topping
   Fresh berries (optional)

1. Simmer milk in double boiler 1 to 2 hours or until milk is light caramel color, stirring occasionally. Pour cooked milk into large bowl. Beat with electric mixer at low speed until milk is smooth and creamy. Bring milk to room temperature.

2. Fold in whipped topping; stir just until smooth. Cover and refrigerate 2 hours or overnight.

3. To serve, divide evenly among dishes. Garnish with berries.

Makes 12 servings

Crispy Battered Plantains

¼ cup sugar

½ teaspoon ground cinnamon

½ cup masa harina, divided

4 large black-skinned plantains, peeled and cut into quarters

1 egg

¼ cup cornstarch

½ cup cold water

Vegetable oil

Vanilla ice cream (optional)

1. Combine sugar and cinnamon in medium bowl; set aside. Place ¼ cup masa harina in small bowl; coat plantains. Set aside.

2. Beat egg in medium bowl. Add cornstarch, remaining ¼ cup masa harina and water, blending until smooth.

3. Heat 1 inch oil in heavy skillet over medium-high heat until oil is 375°F; adjust heat to maintain temperature. Dip plantains in batter, 2 or 3 at a time; fry until golden brown.

4. Drain plantains on paper towels and roll in cinnamon-sugar mixture. Serve warm with ice cream, if desired.

Makes 8 servings

Mexican Wedding Cookies

1 cup pecan pieces or halves
1 cup (2 sticks) butter, softened
2 cups powdered sugar, divided
2 cups all-purpose flour, divided
2 teaspoons vanilla
⅛ teaspoon salt

1. Place pecans in food processor. Process using on/off pulsing action until pecans are ground but not pasty.

2. Beat butter and ½ cup powdered sugar in large bowl with electric mixer at medium speed until light and fluffy. Gradually add 1 cup flour, vanilla and salt. Beat at low speed until well blended. Stir in remaining 1 cup flour and ground nuts. Shape dough into ball; wrap in plastic wrap. Refrigerate 1 hour or until firm.

3. Preheat oven to 350°F. Shape dough into 1-inch balls. Place 1 inch apart on ungreased cookie sheets.

4. Bake 12 to 15 minutes or until golden brown. Let cookies stand on cookie sheets 2 minutes.

5. Meanwhile, place 1 cup powdered sugar in 13×9-inch glass dish. Transfer hot cookies to powdered sugar. Roll cookies in powdered sugar, coating well. Let cookies cool in sugar.

6. Sift remaining ½ cup powdered sugar over sugar-coated cookies just before serving. Store tightly covered at room temperature or freeze up to 1 month.   *Makes about 4 dozen cookies*

Mango Virgin Margaritas

Lime slices and coarse salt

1 large ripe mango, cubed (1¼ to 1½ cups)

1 cup ice

½ cup fresh lime juice

⅓ cup water

¼ cup sugar

3 tablespoons orange juice

1. Rub rim of margarita glasses with lime slices; dip in salt.

2. Combine mango, ice, lime juice, water, sugar and orange juice in blender; blend until smooth. Pour into glasses. Garnish with lime slices.

Makes 2 servings

Rice Pudding Mexicana

1 package (4-serving size) rice pudding

1 tablespoon vanilla

¼ teaspoon ground cinnamon, plus additional for garnish

Dash ground cloves

¼ cup sliced almonds

1. Prepare rice pudding according to package directions.

2. Remove pudding from heat; stir in vanilla, ¼ teaspoon cinnamon and cloves. Divide evenly among dessert dishes.

3. Top with almonds and additional cinnamon. Serve warm.

Makes 6 servings

Prep and Cook Time: 18 minutes

Deep-Fried Ice Cream

1 gallon ice cream, any flavor
12 (8-inch) ORTEGA® Soft Flour Tortillas
4 to 5 cups canola oil, for frying
½ cup granulated sugar
2 teaspoons ground cinnamon

Place plate or sheet pan in freezer. Chill at least 1 hour or overnight.

Form 12 ice cream balls using ice cream scoop. Place on chilled plate. Return to freezer; freeze 1 to 2 hours or until frozen solid.

Brush outside edges of tortilla with water. Place frozen ice cream ball in center of tortilla. Form tortilla around ice cream, using hands to pack it like a snowball. Be sure to enclose ice cream completely and seal well. Return to freezer. Repeat with remaining ice cream balls and tortillas. Freeze at least 3 to 4 hours or overnight.

Heat 3 inches oil in medium saucepan over high heat to 365°F. Line platter with paper towels.

Remove frozen tortilla-covered ice cream balls from freezer, one or two at a time, and carefully lower into hot oil using slotted spoon. Fry 30 to 45 seconds or until golden brown on all sides, turning to color evenly. Remove with slotted spoon. Drain well on paper towels.

Stir together sugar and cinnamon. Roll warm ice cream balls in cinnamon-sugar mixture to coat. Serve immediately. *Makes 12 servings*

Prep Time: **20 minutes**
Start to Finish: **30 minutes**

Toasted Almond Horchata

3½ cups water, divided

2 (3-inch) cinnamon sticks

1 cup uncooked instant white rice

1 cup slivered almonds, toasted*

3 cups cold water

¾ to 1 cup sugar

½ teaspoon vanilla

Ice (optional)

Lime wedges (optional)

To toast almonds, spread in single layer on baking sheet. Bake in preheated 350°F oven 8 to 10 minutes or until golden brown, stirring frequently.

1. Combine 3 cups water and cinnamon sticks in medium saucepan. Cover and bring to a boil over high heat. Reduce heat to medium-low. Simmer 15 minutes. Remove from heat; let cool to temperature of hot tap water. Measure cinnamon water to equal 3 cups, adding additional hot water if needed.

2. Place rice in food processor; process using on/off pulsing action 1 to 2 minutes or until rice is powdery. Add almonds; process until finely ground (mixture will begin to stick together). Remove rice mixture to medium bowl; stir in cinnamon water and cinnamon sticks. Let stand 1 hour or until mixture is thick and rice grains are soft.

3. Remove cinnamon sticks; discard. Pour mixture and remaining ½ cup water into food processor; process 2 to 4 minutes or until mixture is very creamy. Strain mixture through fine-meshed sieve or several layers of dampened cheesecloth into large pitcher. Stir in 3 cups cold water, sugar and vanilla; stir until sugar is completely dissolved.

4. To serve, pour over ice, if desired. Garnish with lime wedges.

Makes 8 to 10 servings

Mexican Hot Chocolate with Chili-Dusted Ice Cream

¾ **cup water**

¾ **cup granulated sugar**

1 **teaspoon ground cinnamon**

1 **heaping tablespoon instant espresso or instant coffee**

 Pinch salt

2½ **squares (2½ ounces) bittersweet chocolate, grated**

2 **cups whole milk**

2 **teaspoons ORTEGA® Chili Seasoning Mix, divided**

1 **teaspoon vanilla extract**

 Vanilla ice cream

Bring water to a boil in medium saucepan. Stir in sugar, cinnamon, espresso and salt. Simmer 1 minute.

Add chocolate; whisk until mixture thickens. Stir in milk, 1 teaspoon seasoning mix and vanilla. Simmer 1 minute.

Serve immediately with dollop of vanilla ice cream sprinkled with ¼ teaspoon seasoning mix.

Makes 4 servings

Prep Time: 5 minutes
Start to Finish: 5 minutes

Tip: You may also make this mixture in advance and reheat it as needed. Before serving, either whisk the mixture well or blend it in a blender to make a light and foamy beverage or dessert.

Tres Leches Cake

1 package (about 18 ounces) white cake mix, plus ingredients to prepare mix

1 can (14 ounces) sweetened condensed milk

1 cup milk

1 cup whipping cream

1 container (8 ounces) whipped topping, thawed

Fresh fruit (optional)

1. Preheat oven to 350°F. Spray 13×9-inch baking pan with nonstick cooking spray.

2. Prepare cake mix according to package directions. Pour batter into prepared pan. Bake 35 to 40 minutes or until toothpick inserted into center comes out clean. Cool in pan 5 minutes.

3. Meanwhile, combine condensed milk, milk and whipping cream in 4-cup measure. Poke holes all over warm cake with toothpick. Slowly pour milk mixture evenly over top of cake. Let cake stand 10 to 15 minutes to absorb liquid. Cover and refrigerate at least 1 hour.

4. Spread whipped topping over cake. Garnish with fruit. Keep cake covered and refrigerated.   *Makes 12 to 15 servings*

Acknowledgments

The publisher would like to thank the companies and organizations listed below for the use of their recipes and photographs in this publication.

California Olive Industry

Campbell Soup Company

ConAgra Foods, Inc.

Del Monte Foods

Dole Food Company, Inc.

Kraft Foods Global, Inc.

National Pork Board

Ortega®, A Division of B&G Foods, Inc.

Reckitt Benckiser Inc.

Riviana Foods Inc.

StarKist®

Unilever

Veg·All®

Index

Index

Metric Conversion Chart

VOLUME MEASUREMENTS (dry)

$^{1}/_{8}$ teaspoon = 0.5 mL
$^{1}/_{4}$ teaspoon = 1 mL
$^{1}/_{2}$ teaspoon = 2 mL
$^{3}/_{4}$ teaspoon = 4 mL
1 teaspoon = 5 mL
1 tablespoon = 15 mL
2 tablespoons = 30 mL
$^{1}/_{4}$ cup = 60 mL
$^{1}/_{3}$ cup = 75 mL
$^{1}/_{2}$ cup = 125 mL
$^{2}/_{3}$ cup = 150 mL
$^{3}/_{4}$ cup = 175 mL
1 cup = 250 mL
2 cups = 1 pint = 500 mL
3 cups = 750 mL
4 cups = 1 quart = 1 L

VOLUME MEASUREMENTS (fluid)

1 fluid ounce (2 tablespoons) = 30 mL
4 fluid ounces ($^{1}/_{2}$ cup) = 125 mL
8 fluid ounces (1 cup) = 250 mL
12 fluid ounces (1$^{1}/_{2}$ cups) = 375 mL
16 fluid ounces (2 cups) = 500 mL

WEIGHTS (mass)

$^{1}/_{2}$ ounce = 15 g
1 ounce = 30 g
3 ounces = 90 g
4 ounces = 120 g
8 ounces = 225 g
10 ounces = 285 g
12 ounces = 360 g
16 ounces = 1 pound = 450 g

DIMENSIONS

$^{1}/_{16}$ inch = 2 mm
$^{1}/_{8}$ inch = 3 mm
$^{1}/_{4}$ inch = 6 mm
$^{1}/_{2}$ inch = 1.5 cm
$^{3}/_{4}$ inch = 2 cm
1 inch = 2.5 cm

OVEN TEMPERATURES

250°F = 120°C
275°F = 140°C
300°F = 150°C
325°F = 160°C
350°F = 180°C
375°F = 190°C
400°F = 200°C
425°F = 220°C
450°F = 230°C

BAKING PAN SIZES

Utensil	Size in Inches/Quarts	Metric Volume	Size in Centimeters
Baking or Cake Pan (square or rectangular)	8×8×2	2 L	20×20×5
	9×9×2	2.5 L	23×23×5
	12×8×2	3 L	30×20×5
	13×9×2	3.5 L	33×23×5
Loaf Pan	8×4×3	1.5 L	20×10×7
	9×5×3	2 L	23×13×7
Round Layer Cake Pan	8×1½	1.2 L	20×4
	9×1½	1.5 L	23×4
Pie Plate	8×1¼	750 mL	20×3
	9×1¼	1 L	23×3
Baking Dish or Casserole	1 quart	1 L	—
	1½ quart	1.5 L	—
	2 quart	2 L	—